JOURNEY
—OF—
FAITH

JOURNEY
OF
FAITH

ENCOURAGEMENT & INSPIRATION
THROUGH LIFE'S CHALLENGES

SERENA M. JOHNSON

PRIMIX
PUBLISHING
THE WRITE CHOICE

Primix Publishing
11620 Wilshire Blvd
Suite 900, West Wilshire Center, Los Angeles, CA, 90025
www.primixpublishing.com
Phone: 1-800-538-5788

All Scripture taken from "Woman's Devotional Bible" Page 80 of my book above was taken from same Bible with a devotional called "Access to God by Gladys Hunt" Page 1233 of the Bible copyright 1990 Zondervan Publishing House. Please see photocopy of these pages with instructions from the "Woman's Devotional Bible".

Published by Primix Publishing: 07/15/2024

ISBN: 979-8-89194-156-4(sc)
ISBN: 979-8-89194-157-1(e)

Library of Congress Control Number: 2024907436

Any people depicted in stock imagery provided by iStock are models, and such images are being used for illustrative purposes only.

Certain stock imagery © iStock.

CONTENTS

Acknowledgements ix
Foreword xi

Life's Experiences 1
Why My Child, Lord? 2
Through the Years 15
Prayer Meetings 29
He is Real! 34
It is So Simple It's Difficult 37
God's Writing On My Hand 42
Keeper of the Well 44
Soaring on Broken Wings 45
Macular Degeneration 49
The Biopsy 52
Minister 73
Catching Up 84
Through Prose 87
Valentine Prayer to Jesus 89
Faith 90
Pathway to God 91
Questions 92
A Generous Spirit 93
Jesus Song 94
Let Jesus In 95
I'll Know I'm Home 96
Angels 97
At The Beach 98

Called 101

Changing Seasons 102

Christmas 103

Christmas Joy 104

Creation 105

Crossing Over 106

Delight in the Lord 107

Giving All 109

Heart Aches 111

Heart to Heart 112

I Am with Thee 115

I Thank Thee, Jesus 117

The Mixture of Marriage 118

More Of You 119

Musings 120

My Abode 121

My Furry Friends 122

Revelation 125

Sing Praises 126

The Flow of Life 127

The Light is There 128

Waves 129

Were You There 130

You'll Never Walk Alone 132

Exercising Faith 133

Get Out of the Boat! 135

Are You Forgiven, Can You Forgive? 136

Gifts 141

Stewardship 145

Onward Christians 147

Debt Has Been Paid 149

New Beginning 151

"Love One Another as I Have Loved You!" 153

Why Me? 155

Inspiration 156

Seeds from Within 157
What is Healing? 159
Is Your Heart Cluttered .162
Is There A Lover In Your House? 164
Thankful for a Change 165
What Vision! 167
What Can We Give? 169
Check Your Gifts. 171
Jesus is the Light 172
War is Ended 175
Independence Day—July 4th 176
There is Joy in the Lord. 178
God's Promise 179
Are You Sleeping? 180
Cleaning Out 181
Are You Filled? 182
It's Free 185
Prayer 186
O Come, Let Us Adore Him, Christ the Lord! 187
Thoughts at Christmas 188
Letter from Santa 189
Eggs? 191
A Tribute to Dorothy Bloom 193
Words of Inspiration and Encouragement 195
I Am With Thee 217

Acknowledgments Index .218

ACKNOWLEDGEMENTS

First and foremost I would like to thank my Mom and Dad, Mary Lillian and Alfred Louis Haddad for bringing me into this world and for their unfailing love and nurturing and pointing me in the right direction. My sister, Judie and brother, Mike, for being supportive of me and caring. My wonderful husband, Don, who has loved me and stood by me through the good times and bad and is such a great blessing to me along with our three children, Shawn, Jodi and Cindy and their spouses. The great joy in our lives are our three grandchildren, Cassidy, Kyran and Mackenzie. We are truly blessed!

My dear friend Joanne, who was the one who led me into this wonderful spiritual adventure through the power of the Holy Spirit. Dennis, Phil and all the dear brothers and sisters of the Agape Fellowship where we were allowed to grow and find our gifts and learn how to use them and our foundation of Biblical teaching and prayer which was priceless. To my Pastors who taught, inspired and encouraged me to be all I can be in the Lord, I will be forever grateful. Many thanks also to my dear friends that have supported, loved and helped me to learn and grow in the Lord.

I would like to dedicate this book to my husband Don, my Mom & Dad, sister Judie, Stacy, Daniel, Evelyn Joe, Kay, Dick, Joanne, Fay, Marge, Angel, Dorothy, Mack, Millie, Joan and Pastor Bob Brookhart, all who have gone home to be with the Lord. Isn't it great to know we will all see each oth4er again one day.

Most of all, this book is dedicated to the Lord, who died in my place, that I may live in Him. For being there always, for loving me always, even when I am unlovable. Without Him, I am nothing. With Him, I am a child of the King of Kings and Lord of Lords!

FOREWORD

This book is a smorgasbord of experiences, insights, prayers and communing with God. Hopefully, they will encourage and help strengthen your relationship with Him.

Nothing has come easy on my walk with the Lord but He has given me joy, peace, love and strength even though I do not deserve it. He has never failed me. He has gotten me through good times and bad. He continues to be there all the time. All I need to do is ask or invite Him to be a part of my day and no matter what happens, He gets me through.

If this book encourages, uplifts, helps or heals you in some way then it's purpose will be fulfilled. May God speak to you in a very special way through these words and may your spirit be open to listen so that you may be blessed.

If you would like to share: Email to smjpray@aol.com

LIFE'S EXPERIENCES

WHY MY CHILD, LORD?

Very softly I heard, "Serena, Serena, wake up!" as I tried to fight my way through the dark clouds of sleep to consciousness. "You have a beautiful baby boy!" The last few wisps dissolved as I opened my eyes. The stark light blinded me and I quickly closed them again. As I squinted them open just a bit, there stood a matronly nurse with her seemingly kind face beaming. "You have a boy, Mrs. Cullen!" she said again. "A boy?" I murmured. "Is he all right?" The nurse then reassured me that my baby was fine, and that he weighed 5 pounds 8 ounces and was 20 inches long. She also informed me that he was a little small, so they placed him in a heated crib, but that he was just fine! "We are going to bring you back to your room," she was saying, as I closed my eyes contentedly and drifted back to the deep voids of sleep.

"Mrs. Cullen . . . . come on now, rise 'n shine. Your lunch will be coming shortly and your husband is waiting to see you." My eyes opened to see the perky nurse trying to straighten my bed. She turned and came back at me with a thermometer. "Come on, open up," she said lightly, as she put it into my mouth. I sat up somewhat and suddenly, as my head cleared a bit, I had so many questions; but I waited until the nurse bustled back, took my pulse and finally took out the thermometer. "I had a boy?" was my first quick question. "Yes," she said, "there's a card over your bed with the weight and all." I then asked, "Where's my husband? Is he here? Can I see him?" "Yes", she replied, "I'll tell him he can come in now, for he's right out in the hall. I'll see you later." I thanked her as she disappeared out of the room. I closed my eyes, not able to think, wanting to drift off again. Suddenly I heard . . . . ."Yep, this must be the place." I jumped as I saw Mike pop his head in the doorway. "Hi, Daddy! Did you see him? It's a boy! Oh, I'm so happy!"

simply rushed out of my mouth. "Yes, I saw him," Mike said. I asked him what our baby looked like. "he is so little they have him in a heated crib in the nursery and you wouldn't believe all the red hair he has. He was wriggling all around, but he didn't open his eyes to see his father," Mike exclaimed. "An old sleepyhead. I can't wait to see him. I still can't believe it's all over . . . that I . . . . me, Serena Cullen, actually had a baby! A real live baby!" "Well you did, Mrs. Cullen, a fine son," Mike said as he squeezed my hand. Excitedly, I said, "We have to give him a name, Mike. Have you been thinking about it? How about Daniel? I really like that. Daniel . . . . Daniel Cullen, that sounds pretty good." "Daniel it is Serena, if that's the name you like, it's ok with me. Now, how about eating something?" Mike said, as the girl came in with my tray. I looked at it, but said I couldn't eat right now for I was too excited. I asked Mike if he called the folks and my sister. He said that he had and that they were all very happy about the baby and that I was fine and that they would be up to see me and the baby as soon as they could.

To go back a bit, so that you understand how the above events came about, when I was nineteen years old I had an argument with my parents before Mike came to pick me up for a date. The anger and rebellion led to a drastic error on my part by having a few drinks and allowing the self-pity to really take control. After just two drinks, which was all that was needed as I did not normally drink at all, my mind was not functioning clearly. We then went to a secluded place to talk well, it was there in the spirit of might as well, they accuse me of it anyway type attitude that I made another devastating mistake. It didn't take long to find out that I was pregnant. I couldn't believe it . . . just one time! The guilt was terrible. I told Mike if he didn't love me, he didn't have to marry me. But he said he did and we were married by a Justice of the Peace. Afterward, our parents insisted that we also get married in the church. So we were also married in the Roman Catholic Church.

After about 2 months of marriage Mike told me he didn't marry me because he loved me, but because he felt he had to, which crushed me. It was really tough going as I wanted this marriage to work. I loved Mike and was looking forward to having the baby. By the time the baby arrived, I had convinced myself that the baby would make all the difference in the world and that everything would be great after that. I really had high hopes that the baby was the answer to everything . . . . that God would forget what happened and all would be great and that I would forget what I had done against God, my parents, myself and everything I had been taught. So, having this baby was really the answer to everything and my hopes were high for the future.

Then the perky young nurse came in and said, "Mr. Cullen, I'm sorry but you'll have to leave now as the babies will be coming out on the floor in a few minutes and Mrs. Cullen needs to rest." Mike then asked me if I wanted him to bring me anything when he returned that evening. I told him I didn't want anything, but for him to come back as soon as he could. He assured me that he would and told me to get some rest and that he would see me later. I said that I would as I watched him almost float out of the room.

There were three other women in the room with me. One was an older lady who had her fifth baby, a girl; her youngest was 16. Another had a girl, her first also; and the third had a son, her second boy. We talked as they all fed their babies. The nurse said that my son would be brought in during the 6 o'clock feeding for me to hold. Finally, I dozed off again.

"Mrs. Cullen, time to wash for supper," is what roused me again. "Ok, nurse", I replied, as I sat bolt upright and, for the first time, I felt really sore. "Ohhhhh," I moaned. "Better not move so quickly," the kind nurse advised. "I'm afraid I just learned that the hard way," I chuckled. We girls chatted away as we washed and waited for our supper. I was famished and gulped down everything in sight. After the supper trays were removed, I could hear wheels in the hallway and babies crying and I thought I would burst from expectation. It seemed like an eternity; all the other girls in the room had their babies already maybe they forgot me! I was starting to worry because they hadn't brought my baby in to me, when suddenly a nurse came in calling, "Mrs. Cullen!" "Right here," I yelled in my eagerness. She smiled and checked our bands, the one on my wrist and the one on his tiny ankle, to make sure they matched. As she started to hand Daniel to me, I asked "How do you hold him, he's so small?" She gently reassured me as she told me to just

4

make sure to keep my arm behind his neck and then she laid him in my arms and briskly marched out.

Oh, he was so cute, wriggling in my arms, so pink and soft wrapped in a little blue blanket. Mike was right, he had a head full of bright red hair. I couldn't help thinking there is an Irishman if I ever saw one! All of a sudden, he started to cry. I was so nervous all thumbs. I didn't know what to do. I had been a babysitter but I had never had one this tiny. He abruptly spit up all over me and himself. "What do I do . . . he just spit up all over! I said, almost in panic. "Just wipe his face and sit him up a bit," one of the girls replied. I was beside myself, and I started to cry. I don't know when I had ever felt so helpless and stupid. "Do you want me to ring for the nurse?" my neighbor in the next bed asked. "Yes, please," I sobbed. When the nurse came in, she compassionately sensed my panic and lovingly took Daniel from my arms saying, "Ok, little guy, we'll stop back and see your Mommy again later, right now you need changing and so does your Mommy. You really did a good job of it." I thanked her as she left and was extremely relieved. I didn't talk much after that as I was so embarrassed. I was nineteen years old and afraid of my own baby! What was I going to do when I got him home? I was really depressed when visiting hours came and Mom and Dad and Mike arrived. They had seen the baby and said he was beautiful. Mom said I'd be somewhat sore but it would go away. Then I broke down and cried. They all asked what was wrong. "I don't know", I retorted. How could I explain to those I love how stupid I felt and how inadequate I was feeling. They probably would have understood, but I just couldn't explain it to them. I didn't want or mean to hurt their feelings, but I just felt lost. I cried off and on all evening, not sleeping much at all.

In the morning, all the routine of the day started, with the taking of temperatures, pulses, baths and heat lamps, taking care of medicines, and the nicest of all, the back rubs. Ohh, they felt heavenly! The nurse had told me that my baby wouldn't be coming in this morning as they didn't want him out of his heated crib too long, but that I would be able to feed him for the first time at the 2 o'clock feeding in the afternoon. I thought, just as well, because I was a little leery after what had happened yesterday. It's a funny feeling for I did look forward to feeding Danny this afternoon.

After breakfast, I started setting my hair to feel a little better about myself and so that Daniel could see his mother looking fairly decent. The curtain was drawn as they were doing something with the girl in the next bed. I heard the doctor's greeting as he entered the room. He pulled the curtain a bit, came in and closed the curtain again. Boy, he looked tired! "don't mind me Doc, I'm making myself beautiful for my son. You look tired. Are we girls giving you a hard time?" He looked at me very sullenly. "Serena", he started. "What's the matter, Doc?", I asked as I became aware of his seriousness. "Serena, something is wrong with the baby." I asked what was wrong. He replied that he was not certain, so he had wanted a Dr. Jones to look at him also, as he was a pediatrician. Would it be all right for Dr. Jones to come in as a consultant. I told him that if he thought it necessary, to contact Dr. Jones. He said it really was necessary and that Dr. Jones was here. He stepped outside the curtain and motioned with his hand for Dr. Jones to come in. As he entered, Dr. Jones said that he would check Daniel over with Dr. Kagan to see what the problem was. After Dr, Jones left, Doc Kagan put his hand on mine and asked if I wanted him to call my mom and have her come to see me. I told him that I would appreciate that, so he said he would call her and he would stop by later as soon as he had some information for me about Daniel.

I wasn't really concerned, as I knew a lot of babies have something wrong with them, like yellow jaundice and other minor ailments, especially ones as small as Daniel. The doctor's would find out what was wrong and take care of it, that's all. I was looking forward to seeing Mom . I'd like a visitor. It was nice of Doc to let me see Mom this early. I wasn't really worried.

In a very short time, Mom arrived. "Hi Mom", I said, cheerfully. "Oh, Serena, I'm so sorry," she blurted out as the tears rolled down her cheeks. She came over to me and hugged me. "Mom, what's wrong? It's ok". Then it hit me like a ton of bricks and I cried, "It's not ok, is it? He's got something real bad, hasn't he?" Mom tried to control herself and sobbed, "Serena, they still don't know what it is but we can still hope and pray he will be all right." I couldn't believe my ears, I just couldn't believe it. God wouldn't let anything happen to Daniel! "I've got to get hold of Mike," I said, as I reached for the phone. Mom said, "Serena, we tried to get him. He's out on his bread route, but his boss is going to try to find him. Come on, let's go out in the waiting room, Serena. Dad is out there and we'll wait for Doc Kagan to let us know how they're doing." I slipped my robe and slippers on and we walked out to the waiting area. There was Dad, red-eyed, trying to conceal the concern and hurt he was feeling. We hugged each other without saying a word. "Serena, are you all right?" he asked. "I'm fine, Dad," I replied. We all sat down at the table, no one saying much, kind of avoiding looking at each other so we could hide our feelings. Maybe we thought the hurt would be easier that way, I don't know. Then my brother-in-law came in. He had left work to come over to the hospital when he found out about the baby.

Shortly afterward, Mike arrived. "How did they get hold of you, Mike?" I asked. "My truck broke down and I called in and my boss told me to wait there and he would pick me up. He didn't tell me about the baby until we were almost in town and he drove me straight here." I told Mike that I was glad that they were able to locate him. Mike went on to say that it was strange that the truck would break down when they were trying to find him and there he was calling into them because of the truck. I replied that it was quite a coincidence. Everyone was so quiet, the tension was unbearable, so I asked Mike to bring us all back some coffee. My nerves were shot. I kept fidgeting. I couldn't keep anymore inside. "When is Doc going to come out," I cried. "I can't stand this waiting!" Mom patted my hand and assured me that Doc would be out soon.

As I looked up, through the tears, I saw Doc coming down the hall. I took one look at his face and screamed, "He's dead, isn't he!" "Serena," Doc said softly. "He is, isn't he!" I screamed again. "Serena, calm down!" he said firmly, "I won't answer anything until you sit down and get hold of yourself!" With this, he summoned a nurse and spoke with her a moment and then she quickly disappeared. "I'm having the nurse get something to help calm you down," Doc said. I was crying uncontrollably. "I don't want anything," I sobbed, "he's dead, I know he is!" The nurse bustled back with a capsule and a glass of water. Doc said, "Serena, take this and then we'll talk." I insisted that I did not want it. Mom pleaded that I take the medication. I took the capsule and the glass from the nurse belligerently and swallowed the capsule. After I practically threw the glass on the table, I said, "Well, Doc, I took the darn capsule . . . . now, what happened?" At this point, I was angry with the whole world. "Serena, Doc replied, "you need that medicine or I wouldn't have given it to you. It will help you somewhat. Yes, you are right. I'm terribly sorry, but he didn't make it." I heard myself scream again, "I knew it! I just knew it! WHY?" I was so beside myself; so bewildered and hurt. Doc gently went on and said, "Serena, we don't know why. Both Dr. Jones and myself tried everything and we still don't know what caused his death. That's why I'd like your permission to do an autopsy to know the cause. Serena, of all the babies I've delivered, this is the first one I've lost, and I don't know why. May I do an autopsy"? I looked at Mike and he shook his head in the affirmative. "Yes," I replied, very forlornly, "you have our permission". Doc then said that he needed someone to verify the death. "I can't," I sobbed. Mom, Dad and Mike went with Doc.

When they returned, I asked Doc if I could go home. I knew I would not be able to stand seeing the other girls babies coming in to be fed. I begged Doc to please let me get out of there for I felt I couldn't take any more. Doc sat and thought for a moment and agreed to let me go, but only if I went to my parents home where someone could be with me all the time. Mom replied that she would be with me if I decided to come home with Dad and her. So it was settled. Mom helped me back to my room and we packed my things together. The girls in the room knew something was wrong when I returned and just said goodbye and good luck to them. They all wished me well.

Everyone was very understanding when I was being discharged and completed all the paperwork and procedures as quickly as possible.

Soon I was in my old room at Mom's and Dad's. They made me change into a nightgown and then into bed. Mom made some coffee and gave me another capsule to take. I insisted again that I did not want it. But Mom persuaded me to take it. We talked for a few minutes as I drank my coffee and then I asked if I could be left alone, as I was very tired. I couldn't sleep right away. As I lay there, the despair I felt was unreal. I kept asking the question over and over again in my mind. Why? Why, God did you do this to me? What did I do to deserve this? Why me? Why my child, Lord? Was it something I did? Is that why you took my baby? I wanted to die. Something in me died anyway. The tranquilizer finally started to take effect and I fell into a fitful sleep I could fight no longer.

Later that evening, Doc Kagan came over. He came into my room with Mom, Dad and Mike to let us know what he had found out. "Serena, I finished the autopsy and found the baby had died from a cerebral hemorrhage. There was a blood vessel in the back of his neck that had frayed and broken, like a rubber band would if it was stretched too tightly." "How? How?" I sobbed quietly. "Serena," he continued, "it wasn't anything you did . . . it just happened! In a way, it is a good thing it happened now, as he could have lived six months or a year and then have gone quite suddenly. Do you understand?" "No, I don't understand. Why did this happen? What have I done? It must have been something I did wrong!" I sobbed. With tears in his eyes, Doc replied, "Serena, I know you are very hurt and upset, but you know I would never mislead you. It had absolutely nothing to do with you. It was in no way your fault! These things happen sometimes. We just don't have all the answers as to why, but I can assure you that nothing you could have done caused the cerebral hemorrhage. Please trust me!" I told Doc that I was sorry, that I knew how much this must hurt him too . . . that I realized that he had been with the baby all day and night and that, here he is with me, when he should be home in bed. I told him that I did believe him, but that I still didn't understand why. "Serena, sometimes it's not for us to understand," Doc said wearily. "I know," I sobbed, "but it might make it easier to take." "I know, Serena, I know. Well dear. I have to go so you can get some rest. I left a prescription with your Mom. You take the medication every four hours and stay in bed for a few days. I want to see you in six weeks, but you call me if you need me." I thanked Doc and he leaned over and kissed me on the cheek. After he left, I couldn't stop crying, I just cried myself to sleep.

The next day was pure torture. The medication kept me pretty well immobile. Mom, Dad and Mike wouldn't let me go to the funeral. I wanted a priest to be there, but I had called two parishes and no one would go because they said it wasn't necessary because the baby was baptized before he died. I was absolutely livid as I felt the church was turning its back on me and my baby when I so desperately needed support.

Resentment kept building with God and with the Church.

So many questions were whirling around in my head. Why did I deserve this? Was I such a terrible person? Why so much pain? Yes, I've made mistakes, maybe I haven't always done what's right, but have they been that bad? Was this the ultimate price I had to pay by you, God? Taking my baby from me? You are not a merciful God! I hate you for what you have done to me!

After much discussion, my parents finally relented and consented to let me go home to our apartment, telling Mike to take good care of me. As we entered the apartment to the kitchen, the door was open which led to the room we had done over for the baby. My eyes caught sight of the cute animals on the wallpaper and the crib set up in the corner with the sheets all on and the beautiful quilted comforter I had received at the huge shower that was given for me a few weeks before.

Mike said, "Don't go in there. I guess I should have removed everything as your mother suggested but I walked in anyway. I glanced at the gifts I hadn't finished sorting on the newly painted bureau. Like a magnet, I was drawn to the crib. "Why, Mike, why did this have to happen?" I sobbed. "His beautiful crib he never even got a chance to use." Completely overwhelmed in self-pity and grief, I lay over the side of the crib on folded arms and broke down. Mike finally came over and steered me toward the door and into our bedroom where I lay on the bed and cried myself to sleep.

When I awoke, I asked Mike if he would mind if I let my sister borrow all the baby things as she had her first child a few weeks before and hadn't had a shower and could use everything I had. He said he didn't mind so I called her and she agreed she could use them and would be grateful to be able to borrow them for a while. Mike packed all the clothing and everything else for the baby and took it to my sister's home. When he returned, I asked him how our nephew was. "He's doing fine and your sister said to come over real soon to see her and the baby." Mike said. "That would be hard for me, Mike but I suppose I have to get used to seeing other babies sometime, I guess I can't avoid it forever."

The next day and very often after that, I did go to my sister's and she was very understanding of my situation as she let me hold her baby as often as I wanted. It was difficult at first and I guess I spoiled my nephew a bit, but it helped me so much to be able to at least hold a baby and to be so happy for someone else. I must admit I had twinges of jealousy at times.

Christmas time was especially hard for me all I could think of while at my sister's was that my baby would be as big as hers, and that we would have had a joyous Christmas together too. All I could think of was why was he taken from me? When we returned to our apartment, Mike dropped me off and he went to work. After he left, all I felt was pain and hurt. Sitting, remembering my nephew, I suddenly had to find my baby. I thought I love him I'll tell him. I was oblivious to the cold and the snow as I walked falteringly across the busy road in front of our apartment and wandered into the cemetery which was across the street. Our baby had been buried there at the feet of my grandmother. My coat wide open, no hat or boots, I frantically tried to find my baby. I brushed the snow off tombstone after tombstone, looking desperately for Gram's name. Between the snow and the tears, I couldn't find the grave. It was an impossible task. I finally fell, exhausted, in the soft cool snow. As I lay there sobbing, a man came up to me. "Young lady, what on earth are you doing here on a night like this?" He startled me and it took a few moments for me to speak, but finally I blurted out, "I'm trying to find my baby." He asked, "Do you live far from here?" No, just across the street," I said very softly. "Well you best be getting home and come back some other time." He said. I hesitantly got to my feet and somehow obediently started home. How I ever managed to get across the road both ways without being hit by a car, I'll never understand, as my grief was so strong I never even thought about looking to see if one was coming.

As I walked up the steps, I started to shiver and finally became aware of how bitter cold it was and that it was snowing quite hard. I opened the door shaking, sobbing and covered with snow. I took off my coat automatically, went into the bedroom, closed the door, and cried until I was so exhausted, my mind went blank and sleep crept in to comfort me.

A few months passed. I had tried to convince myself that all had happened for the best. I finally got a job and made many new friends at work. Generally, everything was all right until I found that I was pregnant again. Through the whole pregnancy, I worried. My mind was in a constant upheaval and very often I cried.

It was one of the better evenings, as Mike and I had joked together, and I went to bed content. During the night, I got up with cramps, which I thought was gas. I tried to walk off the gas but couldn't, Then it dawned on me that maybe I was in labor, but it just didn't seem strong enough. I woke Mike up and called the doctor. "Serena," Doc said, "get right to the hospital. I'll meet you there." We both got dressed and rode to the hospital.

I was frightened, I couldn't help thinking, the same thing may happen to this baby. As soon as I was checked in, they examined me and brought me directly to the delivery room. Within minutes, before they could give me anything, the baby was born. "A boy, Serena," Doc Kagan said. They gave me a shot of something and before I knew it, I was out cold.

When I awoke, Mike was there. "Is he ok?" I asked. Mike replied softly, "Yes, he's a big one 7 lbs., 8 oz. and yes, he's ok". "Is he in a heated crib", I asked, as I was still unsure. "No, Serena, please don't worry. Doc says he's fine." Mike said as he tried to reassure me, but I was still quite apprehensive. However, as the days passed and we took our son home, that heavy feeling began to leave. I thanked the Lord for our beautiful, healthy, baby boy. He had taken one, but had performed the miracle of giving us another and we all had a chance at a new beginning. I had for a time turned my back on God at a time I needed Him most.

Sometimes we learn through experience. It took this sad event to have me look to God for help. I had many other equally traumatic experiences thus far in my life which God has gotten me through. But, I had never given the credit where credit is due. I alone could not have handled these situations, but with God, all things are possible! I have also learned that God never leaves you nor forsakes you , you are the one who turns your back on Him. He was there all the time and I just went to Him in times of trouble. The rest of the time, I did what I wanted to do. When I was in total control of my life, things didn't go too well; but when God intervened, I took most of the credit. I might have referred to God, but I hogged the glory. I found the most important truth in my life and I'd like to share it with you.

A friend told me that Jesus Christ (whom I had heard all about and believed in), loved me so much . . . . ME!! That He died on the cross in my place FOR MY SIN. If I was the only person to ever live on this earth, He would have done it just for ME. Well, He did it just for me and for YOU too. He loves you so much He gave His life for YOU. He loves you JUST AS YOU ARE. You don't have to be 6 feet tall or weigh 125 pounds or have blonde hair or beautiful teeth or a person who has done nothing but good all your life (but He loves them too). HE LOVES YOU JUST THE WAY YOU ARE. HE DIED FOR YOU!! After three days, He rose from the dead and sits at the right hand of the Father. HE'S ALIVE!! The Son of God, Jesus Christ is alive and all you have to do is repent (or turn away from your sin), ask His forgiveness and invite Him to be Lord (take control) of your life. Surrender it all to Him, for the only way to the Father is through His Son, Jesus Christ. Then, you are born of His Spirit. Ask Him to fill you to overflowing with His Spirit so you may know what His plan for your life is and then read the Bible so you may know how He lived and let the Holy Spirit teach you about Jesus and what He would have you do.

If you sincerely desire this relationship with Jesus, why not ask Him now to be Lord of your life and you will find that if you yield yourself to Him, He will show you what He would have you do and, oh, what peace and joy and excitement are yours as a child of the King of Kings. If you are sincere, you will know that you are truly Born Again when you see the evidence which may be, that all of a sudden you aren't swearing anymore or that your want to's, that were not God's way, are changing into the want to's, that line up with God's Word. Then, as you learn more about Jesus and try to please Him, the more your life is enriched and blessed for you cannot out give God. After a while you will truly know that "All things work to the good of them that love God and are called according to His purpose".

THROUGH THE YEARS

I have contemplated writing a story. Well, not really a story but telling circumstances in my life that may help someone to understand the subject of this book. Things that I have had happen that are very weird, which I call weird, but are they really? It is my hope that in the coming chapters that you will find some insight, inspiration, love and caring which I have found in my Lord and Savior, Jesus Christ. As you are reading there will probably be some things you may not believe. I know there were a lot of things I did not believe. But if you open your heart and open your eyes and open your ears and ask God to lead you and show you, He will show you the truths that are in this book. Hopefully, they may change your life as they have mine. There is one thing I will share with you before you even begin . . . you're going to think it's pretty weird. You know what? It's changed my life so drastically, that I know in all that I have been through and all that I will go through that there is someone that sticketh to me closer than a brother and there is someone who loves me no matter what I have done or said. Or, no matter how I have blown it there is always forgiveness, if I would just turn to Him. So, you're probably going to laugh because God has a real sense of humor. In some of the instances I have found myself in I still look back and laugh and that's the joy of the Lord. They say we're fools for Christ . . . yes, we do have fun. Whoever said being a Christian is tough, do not get me wrong it is at times but there is such joy and such freedom. We don't need to drink or take drugs to get high. We don't need all the things the world has to offer to get joy. We can have the joy of the Lord no matter what the circumstances or what the pain, if we but look to Him. So here goes hope you enjoy hope it's a blessing to you .

I was born the second child of Mr. & Mrs. Alfred L. Haddad on December the 14th, 1941 which was 7 days after Pearl Harbor was attacked. When I was born it was a hard time as Dad was working as a shoe salesman in Bristol, Connecticut.

When I was approximately 6 months old we moved to Pittsfield, Massachusetts where my dad worked with my uncles in my grandfather's Oriental rug store along with my Mom. We were relatively poor and had to pinch pennies but our life was good our family was around us. My sister Judie is the oldest, a year and a half older than me and I was supposed to be a boy, Michael but it didn't turn out that way. They had not picked a girl's name but Dad had been reading a book with the name Serena in it. Both Mom and Dad liked the name so they named me Serena but I was nicknamed Mike till my brother came along. Mom had a miscarriage a year or two after I was born it was another girl. But, alas, 5 years later my brother Michael was born that completed our family.

When we were young my dad started a business. It was a variety store and lunch counter and we sold patent medicines, cards, magazines, some groceries and every day essentials along with an ice cream and soda fountain. Although, it seems, after they bought the business, family life just wasn't the same. The store was open 7 days a week from 7 in the morning till 11 o'clock at night, so there was always somebody missing as they had to tend the store. All my life I have been in a rushed world always busy. Mom and Dad worked real hard to provide us with things. They loved us and gave themselves for us . . . I was proud of Mom & Dad. Mom made sure we always went to church on Sunday even if they couldn't go because they were working in the store. As I was growing up I loved God with all my heart. There were times I went to the Catholic Church by myself and just talked to God. I sometimes wondered if He heard me but I loved Him. The one thing I remember that I was taught in catechism was the question,

"Who was God? God is all over, sees all things and hears all things." I believe that. As I grew older, because I did not understand the Masses as they were said in Latin, I just couldn't go to Mass. I would leave the store to go to Mass and stop at another store and have coffee during the Mass and come back when it was over. But I still went to church when there wasn't a Mass and would talk to God.

My teenage years were hard. I worked in the store and there were a lot of things I missed. Like being able to do after school activities etc. I was always sick with bronchitis, ear infections, strep throats, many things . . . out of school many days. I graduated from High School and went to work for New England Telephone and Telegraph as a telephone operator. I thoroughly enjoyed my job, as I really loved people. During this time we bought another store and for a while we had two stores in which I worked besides going to work as an operator.

As a teenager I was looking for love; I needed to know that someone really cared for me. Oh, I knew my mother and father did, but it always seemed like my sister, who was the first child and grandchild, was more important and so was my brother, the first and only son and grandson. I was the middle child, which many that read this book will relate to. One night I had an argument with my mom and dad and I was really mad when I went out. They had accused me of doing things that I had never thought of doing. I then went on a date with my boyfriend and had a few drinks which is something that I normally did not do and between the anger and the drink, it was my downfall. I had made a big mistake, all it takes is once. Several weeks later I suspected I was pregnant and it turned out that I was correct. I told the father, he did not have to marry me if he didn't want to but he did. This was a very tough time in my life. We got married by a justice of the peace. My mom and dad insisted we get married by the church so we had another ceremony a few weeks later by a priest. Several weeks after we got married my husband said that he only married me because of the baby, he didn't marry me because he loved me. I was devastated but told myself he didn't mean it. He would leave almost every night and go eat at his parents house leaving me alone to fend for myself for food. He quit his job and he would meet his parents at a bar at night and drink with them. He would then come home drunk and verbally and physically abuse me. I truly believed I had married for better or worse before God and I kept hoping things would change especially after the baby was born. One night, during the winter, as we were going out to go to the bar to see his parents, my husband was in a rush as we were a bit late. We had a second floor apartment and while rushing down the stairs. I slipped and fell about halfway down catching the railing with my hand near the bottom. I was about 6 or 7 months pregnant. All my husband said as he was opening the car door was hurry up, get up and get in the car we are late. So I just got up and went but was very sore.

When the baby was born we named him Daniel, everything was good . . . the next morning I was supposed to be able to hold him and see him for the first time . . . well I did hold him but I couldn't feed him as he could not be out of the incubator for a long time. He was beautiful, with a head full of bright red hair and a cherub face. He was so tiny and squirmy, I did not know what to do as he was so small to hold. He upchucked on me and I called the nurse and she had to take him back. I just laid and cried wondering how I could ever take care of a baby. Then the next day I was going to be able to feed him. As I was setting my hair, I wanted to look good for my baby when he saw me again, the doctor came in and said "Serena, there is something wrong with the baby." "That's alright, you'll take care of it," I said. "I have a doctor with me who is a pediatrician. I would like to have him look at the baby too if that is ok with you" said Doc. So the pediatrician went in to look at him. My doctor said "Do you want me to call your mother?" Why not, it wasn't visiting hours and I would like to see my mother. Well, Mom came, when she saw me her face dropped and the tears flowed as she walked over to my bed and said "I'm sorry." So I tried to comfort her, "It's alright Mom, he's going to be ok". She said "Serena it's serious." "Yes, but he's going to be alright", I said. "I don't know," she said. "He's got to be alright," I cried. To make a long story short, he wasn't. After 2 ½ days he went to be with Jesus. I was devastated. He died of a cerebral hemorrhage . . . the vein in the back of his head was frayed like a rubber band. The doctor wanted me to go to my parents home to recover, so I did. This was a devastating time in my life as my husband was still drinking heavily and did not want to work. I became pregnant again right away. When I found out I was pregnant again I was really afraid the same thing would happen to this new baby.

God had taken away my first born but was giving me another.

When Shawn was born on December 20th, 1963, he was over 7 lbs. and very healthy. I was able to take him home on Christmas Day! God's gift to me. I was so protective of him and watched him very closely so that nothing could happen to him, as did his brother. My husband was still drinking heavily and came home one night and started yelling and woke up the baby. I went to pick him up to comfort him and as I held Shawn in my arms my husband grabbed his two hands and jerked him from me. He was about 5 months old. Something snapped within me. I yelled at him that he had done all he wanted to me but he was not going to hurt my baby. I took Shawn from him and laid him down in the crib and just pounded my husband on the chest yelling at him to leave us alone. Well, he got mad and stomped out. I called my Mom & Dad and told them what had happened and asked if I could go there. They said yes, so the next morning I left with the baby and our clothes and what my family had given us as wedding presents. My husband had abused me but he was not going to abuse my baby. I was mad at God, I was mad at the world, I was mad at everybody. I was so hurt.

I went back to live with Mom & Dad and I was so mentally hurt I couldn't even take care of Shawn. So, I worked in my Mom & Dad's store and let Mom take care of him. I would scream at him as I could not stand his crying . . . yet I loved him dearly. A divorce is a tragic thing, being abused and unloved is a tragic thing. I did not know what to do, where to go, who to turn to. I went to the church for help that I could get an apartment of my own and they turned me down they said I had done the right thing by leaving my husband but they could not help me.

One day while I was working in the store this fellow came in and I started talking to him and he was very nice, very quiet. He came in several times and we got to know each other a bit. One day he asked me out and I said no because I had filed for a divorce and it wasn't final yet and I did not want anything to get in the way of me having full custody of my child. I would give no reason for my husband or anyone else to say I wasn't a fit mother. My husband had committed adultery several times, so I found out, and I did not want my son taken away from me. Don every so often would ask me again to go on a date and the only thing I could do was have him come upstairs and watch TV or play cards while my Mom or Dad was there. When we finally did go out, most of the time we took my son with us.

On December 17, 1965, Don and I were married. I was still working because I wanted to pay off the divorce myself. I would put Shawn in a day care center which was very difficult. Before we were married my x-husband agreed to let Don adopt Shawn if he could stop paying child care. So very soon after our marriage Don adopted Shawn and we gave Shawn a middle name, Donald. I was so thrilled that Don loved Shawn so much he wanted to give him his name which was an honor. Within a short time I discovered I was pregnant and 9 months and 10 days after we were married our daughter Jodi arrived. Her birth was not without trepidation as during the delivery I was asked to stop pushing as the cord was wrapped around her neck. Thank God, I was able to stop and they got the cord unwrapped and she was just fine. What a joyous occasion that was for all of us. A beautiful little girl for us to love and a baby sister for Shawn.

Five months after Jodi was born I suddenly had an extreme pain in my stomach it was so severe I was in a fetal position writhing in pain. The doctor came to the house (Yes, they did house calls then) and had to pry me loose to examine me. He determined it was a gallbladder attack and gave me a shot to relieve the pain and relax me. I had X rays and they determined it indeed was my gallbladder and that I needed to have it out as soon as possible before I suffered another attack. The day I was supposed to find out about the X rays and tests . . . Don came home from work early and said pack me a bag I have to go into the hospital today! I was flabbergasted . . . what for? Apparently he started bleeding at work and went to our regular doctor at noon time and he called a specialist and sent him right over there from his office and the specialist said the bleeding was from hemorrhoids but they were gangrenous and had to be removed immediately before the infection spread. While packing his bag I got the phone call that I need to be admitted to the hospital as soon as possible to have my gall bladder removed. Meanwhile, I had a 3 year old and a 5 month old child to take care of. Well I brought my husband to the hospital and he had his surgery and then he developed a high fever . . . had developed some kind of infection and was really sick. Finally, with antibiotics he was able to come home . . . . he was home recuperating less than two weeks and I had to go in for my surgery. When I came home 10 days later I could not pick up anything for 6 weeks . . . so had to have a neighbor change Jodi from bed to playpen and then Don would put her in bed at bedtime. What a difficult time that was.

Within three years I was pregnant for Cindy. Cindy I almost lost, I didn't want another baby, I did not think I could handle it mentally. Then I almost lost her when I was 7 months pregnant, I started bleeding and ended up in the hospital for 3 days wondering if I was going to lose her or not and I cried out to God that I really did want her and I was truly sorry for saying or thinking I didn't. I pleaded with God to keep her safe and well and let me have this baby. Finally, I stabilized and I was able to go home. I ended up three times going to the hospital in the 9th month, two times for false labor and the third time she was born, beautiful and whole. After she was born the doctor showed me the placenta and it looked like a large steak with a white bone in it. He explained that if the placenta had not closed in around the white part I would have lost the baby, and that I was very fortunate. By the grace of God I had our second beautiful baby girl.

Soon after Cindy was born I would have miscarriage after miscarriage for a few years which was taking its toll on me mentally and physically. Just before Christmas I was cleaning house and moved our couch to clean and vacuum underneath and I was in pain and bleeding. Don took me to the doctor and he said I was pregnant and sent me to a gynecologist who confirmed this and that I had to have a D & C as I was miscarrying once again. When we arrived at the hospital they tried to give me what they call a saddle block, they tried 3 times and it did not take, for as the doctor was doing the D & C, I felt it all, as he scraped and had to dig out the intrauterine device I had inside so I would not get pregnant. I screamed and the doctor told the anesthesiologist why do you insist on this kind of anesthesia it does not work? After the procedure, I had to stay overnight and I was a nervous wreck and blaming myself. I did not know I was pregnant and I would not have moved the couch if I had known. That it was my fault the baby died. Within a few months after that I was having problems again and went to another gynecologist and he said I was pregnant again but that I would never carry the baby full term because my insides were a mess. I would never be able to carry another child full term and I should have a hysterectomy. Due to the fact I could not physically or mentally keep going through this, we agreed to the surgery. The day I went in for the surgery I miscarried. I was devastated by the whole thing. I could never have another child and I had lost yet another one. At least it would not keep happening.

All of these things laid heavily on my mind. I couldn't stand my kids talking to me, I was always in the house, I couldn't do anything. I was miserable. One day my sister came and talked to me and said if you won't do it for yourself do it for everybody else . . . you have to get some help!

At that time my oldest daughter was having problems in school and I was called in to talk with the school psychologist. She was finishing her work quickly and then talking and bothering the others and they could not finish their work. Always busy, busy. So we met a few times and he discussed how I could make her sit in a corner when she would not behave for a few minutes. I also discussed my problems and why I might have been lax at the discipline and asked if he knew where I might get some help that we couldn't afford a lot of money. He suggested a mental health clinic, which I finally called and made an appointment. I went on and off for about a year, just to talk things out. Sometimes after an appointment I would go out and sit in the car and cry for a while before I could drive home. She really helped me sort out some of my feelings, mostly by listening and letting me know things that happened were not my fault.

I started working while the children were in school, just part time. I had an Avon lady that lived in the neighborhood and we became friends. I would stop after work and have a cup of coffee and talk. She had a problem with her back and wore a steel brace. She could not sit or stand for more than a few minutes without excruciating pain. She had to lay on the floor to get her canned goods out of the cabinets. The doctors told her it would only get progressively worse, nothing else they could do. I used to pray with her sometimes, lay my hands on her shoulders and pray. She said she used to feel better but it would come back.

This one day she called and said she had met some people that told her of a healing service in Boston, a Father McDonough and she was going. I said "Great!. I believed God could heal her". After she came home from the service she called me and said she had been healed! No more brace, no more pain. I said that is nice, great! But, kind of wondering if it was real. She asked me to stop by for coffee after work so I could see for myself. For some reason I cannot explain, it took me about three weeks to get there and when I did there was a friend of hers there. She said "I'm sorry I am just leaving but Joanne would you pray for my son before I go?" Joanne said "Sure," and introduced Alicia to me and asked, "Serena, will you pray with us?" I said "sure." So we all joined hands and Joanne started to pray. A very nice prayer when all of a sudden she started praying funny, I mean it sounded like Chinese. I really wanted to laugh as she sounded so funny but I knew I shouldn't as we were praying to God, so I held it in. As soon as she finished I burst out laughing and said "Joanne, what were you doing? You were praying and all of a sudden you sounded so funny?" She said "Oh!" Alicia said to Joanne, "I've got to go, I will talk to you later, nice to meet you, Serena." Joanne said "Serena I'll explain in just a minute" I said "Ok, goodbye Alicia" and Joanne walked Alicia to the door. I was really anxious to hear why she had sounded so funny, so when Joanne came back into the kitchen. I laughed again and said "Ok, what is the story?" She told me she was praying in the Spirit and that it was a direct pipeline to God. I went from laughing, to wanting it with all my heart. I asked how I could get that, that I loved God and wanted to be as close as possible to Him. She explained to me that we are all sinners and needed a savior and that Jesus, the Son of God came as a man, was born of a virgin in a manger, grew up and ministered to people in the WORD and healed many sick and taught about God the Father and then He took all the sin upon Himself for me at the cross where He was crucified and died. He was buried for 3 days and then He rose from the dead and said He was going to the Father but He would send His Holy Spirit to comfort us and guide us. And that one day He would be coming back again to earth to gather His people to Him. She asked me if I believed all this and I said yes, I did. She asked me if I wanted to ask Jesus to forgive my sins and ask Him into my heart to be my Lord and Savior? Which I readily did. Then she prayed that I receive the baptism of the Holy Spirit with evidence of speaking in tongues (praying in the Spirit). I felt like a heavy weight lift off of me and Joanne told me about her healing and showed me how she could bend and stand and no pain. I was thrilled. I did not however, get the tongues and Joanne told me to go home and to keep praying it would be in God's timing. For three days I tried, I cried out to God . . . told Him I was sorry for laughing at Joanne while she was praying but I did not understand what it was. I would get a deep groaning inside but thought it was me. I opened my mouth and would ask Him to fill it. After the third day of trying, when the kids were in school and my husband at work, I was really upset I hadn't got it yet. I walked over to Joanne's house and knocked on her door. When she answered, there was no hello or anything, I just shouted at her, "I thought you said all I had to do was ask and I would receive it!" "Calm down, Serena, come in and we'll discuss it." Joanne explained to me that sometimes there were hindrances that blocked the receiving . . . like, did I ever play with a ouiji board or have my palm read or read horoscopes. I had done all these things at one time or another and I told her yes, but I did not believe them. She said well, that all had to do with the devil and what I had to do was tell Satan I wanted no part of him or his works and for him to get out of my life as I was a child of the King, Jesus. Then I was to ask Jesus for forgiveness for being involved in any way with Satan. Then ask Jesus again for the gift. I said OK, bye and left. I wanted the gift so bad I couldn't wait . . . I wanted all God had for me. I ran home, into the house, up the stairs, knelt down beside my bed and said "Satan, I do not want any part of you, I belong to the Lord Jesus Christ, you get out of my life for good. I am covered by the blood of the Lamb. Be gone in the Name of Jesus! Jesus, I am so sorry for involving myself in those things that were not of you, the ouiji board and horoscopes, a woman read my palm on a boardwalk and my aunt using a thread and needle to see if I would have boys or girls when I had children. Forgive me, Lord, for looking to anyone else or anything else, other than you. Make me white as snow. I am completely yours in Jesus' Name. Lord, I really want all of you, I know I laughed when I heard tongues for the first time but I did not know what they were, I really want all that you have for me. Fill me with your Spirit." Then, as I gave my voice over to Him the prayer language just started flowing and I could stop it any time I wanted and start it up again. WOW! I prayed in the Spirit and cried knowing that the Holy Spirit was inside me praying to the Father. A direct line to God. Wow! God is so good. After about an hour of praying, praising and crying I called Joanne and told her I got it! I got it! She was excited with me and we both praised the Lord on the phone and laughed about my going over her house the way I did. Thank God she was so understanding. I was so hungry for God, I couldn't wait.

Well that was the turning point in my life. I started going to a prayer group with Joanne which was called Agape Fellowship. That was weird! The first time I went I thought, these people are a little strange. They were very nice to me but there was just something different about them. They praised the Lord and raised their hands and sang hymns and praise songs to Jesus. It was nice and I wanted to praise God too, but felt self-conscious. Then the leader announced anyone who wanted prayer to come forward. Well, we all came forward and they were putting oil on their heads and praying. The first lady he prayed for fell on the ground . . . scared me half to death . . . I thought she had a heart attack or something. Joanne said to me, she is alright she is just resting in the Spirit . . . RIGHT! Her eyes were fluttering so she was alive. She finally got up and said she was fine, that she felt wonderful. Jesus had healed her. Okkkkkkk . . . Nobody was the least bit concerned . . . just praising the Lord she was healed. Strange . . . Well, after that incident I did not go again for about 3 weeks. Weird people. I talked to Joanne on the phone though and finally I decided I'd try again. This night after praising and singing and teaching from the scriptures, the leader Dennis asked if there was anyone who wanted to dedicate themselves totally to God and surrender all to Him. Would they come forward for prayer. I wanted that more than I had ever wanted anything in my entire life, so I went forward. He asked me if I had accepted Jesus as my Lord and Savior and I told him yes, I had. He put oil on my head and he and the other prayer group members put their hands on my shoulders and back and prayed for me. I fell down but someone was behind me and let me down gently and I could not move, I felt such a peace come over me almost like waves and I really did not want to move, I wanted to feel the peace, I did not want it to go away. Finally I got up and I understood what happened to Kay several weeks ago and why no one was concerned. God bless the members of this Agape Fellowship, for with their help I was able to grow so much more in the Lord than I had been able to at my church. I learned all about the gifts of the Spirit and the fruits of the Spirit and how to walk in the Spirit. Through reading scripture, hands on learning, experiencing correction and direction as the Bible teaches through the power of the Holy Spirit and discovering who I am in Christ. This prayer group was very instrumental in my deep walk and understanding of the Lord Jesus and His love for me through others with true, all-encompassing Agape love.

At the time of this happening to me, we were members of an American Baptist Church and I was so excited about what God had done in my life, I wanted everyone to experience it. It did not take long to find out not everyone believed in the gifts and not everyone believed in what the Bible says. That was a shock to me. I was causing quite a stir in my church because I was so on fire for Jesus. Oh they were happy that I was more dedicated and did a lot more in church on various committees and that I was the editor of the newsletter and was teaching Sunday school and even being a counselor for camp and going with the youth to state conventions.

Now here, I must digress . . . I have always loved God as far back as I can remember, always was involved in the church. Had even taken on contacting doctors and hospitals in the area to get samples of drugs and supplies to go to Managua, Nicaragua as one of the Pastors in the area, Rev. Christialite was flying there in his plane. My husband and I had also picked up the medical supplies and clothing donations and got them ready for him to bring with him.

Through the Sunday school class, which included two of my children, all of them had accepted the Lord Jesus as their Savior and all were baptized in water. At the summer camp I was a counselor and it was the first time I had ever been to camp in my life. I knew nothing. But, Pastor Foulk showed me what I needed to do and helped me to accomplish it as he was the director for the time I was there. That was such an enriching experience for me as I was able to lead one of the girls in my cabin to the Lord and just enjoy the fellowship. We had to do a skit for one of the nights at campfire and it was so funny I wet my pants laughing. I had to make a run for it. I was so embarrassed but no one really knew. I just loved being where the Lord is and talking about Him and sharing Him with others.

While at this church, many thought I had gone off the deep end. There were some who did not believe in the Baptism of the Holy Spirit or praying in the Spirit. They said it was not for today. I could not believe that as I had experienced it first hand and it was real! I could not understand why they could not just go to God and ask Him. That is what I did. I even asked that we could use a room in the church building for our prayer meetings as we were temporarily out of a meeting place. Well, we met there for a while and then it was heard that people were being "slain in the Spirit" and singing and dancing and praising the Lord for hours and they did not want us there.

Yes, all those things were happening but it was the power of God working. This was a non-denominational group with several denominations represented and all were welcome to come. Many wonderful things happened. I remember one night we were holding hands in a circle praying and all of a sudden my hands started burning (the palms). I told the lady next to me that my hands were burning terrible, what should I do? She said tell Dennis. (the leader) . . . so I told Dennis . . . and he announced to everyone, anyone that needs prayer come up and Serena will lay hands and pray. I said what? I don't know how or what to do and Kay said just put your hand on them and say whatever comes to your mind . . . God will help you He is anointing you for prayer. So a man came up I went to lay my hand on him and he fell to the floor. I almost did too. But I prayed for him and I prayed for others and that was my first experience under the anointing to pray for others. One night we had a Prophetess come and speak and she prayed over each of us and she confirmed a healing ministry for me and that I would be a Prophetess and have a hard time ahead. All I knew was I wanted to follow Jesus and do what He wanted me to do.

PRAYER MEETINGS

Joanne invited me to a prayer group where she had met some people who directed her to Father McDonough's healing service, where the Lord healed her back. Well, I went to the prayer meeting. The people were very friendly, very nice, and very loving as she introduced me to each one. The prayer meeting started and everyone started singing, which was great and they were praising the Lord, some of them with their hands up in the air and their eyes closed. Then the leader asked for anyone who needed a healing and wanted prayer to come up front. Most of us went up and he was going to lay hands on us and pray. As we were just standing there and praising the Lord and praying I saw a woman to the left of me just fall right down on the ground. I thought she had a heart attack or something but nobody seemed to be upset about it but I was, along with another girl who was there for the first time. They told us it was all right that there was nothing wrong that the Holy Spirit had just touched her and was working on her. Well, after a few minutes she got up off the floor and she seemed to be fine. She thought it was just great. The leader and others explained to us about what being "slain in the Spirit" was or "falling under the power of the Holy Spirit". What a revelation that was! Well to make a long story short, after that meeting I was not sure whether I wanted to go back again and it was a long time before I did. Something just kept drawing me back. The thing that was drawing me was the love. The love of Jesus that I felt there, the encouragement, the caring. They loved me for me, they did not care what my past was, what my present was, they just loved me anyway and that is the greatest feeling anyone can ever experience. If you have ever experienced these things and thought the people were weird, I challenge you to go and try it again, but most of all allow them to bring you into a saving knowledge of the Lord Jesus Christ that you may feel His power and His presence and you can share in His love and the love the body of Christ have for each other. There is nothing quite like it. You may love your family, you may love your husband but this is a different kind of love, an all encompassing love, no matter what, you're ok. It's very easy to have this, all you have to do is accept Jesus. Tell Him that you are sorry that you have sinned and ask His forgiveness, ask Him to come in to your heart and be Lord of your life and He will. Ask Him to baptize you in the Holy Spirit that you may have everything that He wants you to have, that you may go forth in His Name, that He may cleanse you from all unrighteousness and that He may show you the way He would have you walk, and help you to obtain it. That He will give you encouragement through the body of Christ, your brothers and sisters who are there to help you, to nurture you and bring you into a fuller knowledge of the Lord Jesus Christ. It's the most rewarding, marvelous joy you could ever experience and He never leaves you nor forsakes you. No matter how gloomy it may get in this world, He's always there with you. If you but look to Him, you are never alone.

Since that meeting, I have been to many, many prayer groups in which I have been totally blessed. The one that comes to mind where again we had been singing and praising the Lord and the leader felt led to start praying for the sick. Well, first we held hands and started praying, we prayed in tongues, we prayed in English as the Lord led us. As we were praying my hands started burning, they were really burning so bad. Kay was on my right and I believe Dennis was on my left. My hands were so hot you could feel the heat coming from my hands. I looked down at my hands and I really couldn't understand it. I said to Kay. "My hands are really burning terribly.!" I looked at them and in the middle of my hands there was a big square of white on each palm and the rest of the hand was red and they burned. I said to Kay, "My hands are burning so bad I do not know what to do with them and I rubbed them on my legs and Kay said something to Dennis and he said "Oh, you have an anointing, start praying for people." He said "Ok, who needs prayer come over and let Serena pray with you as she is anointed. This fellow mentioned he needed prayer and came over to me. I said "I do not know how to pray for people". Dennis said "When they come up all you do is lay hands on them and pray for them. Let the Lord give you the words. Let the Holy Spirit guide you as you pray. Ask them what they need prayer for and just pray with them." Well, the man came up and told me what he needed prayer for and I went to lay my hands on him and he went boom, right down on the floor! I did not know what to do, it scared me. I asked, "How could this happen? I didn't even hardly touch him and he went down on the floor." Dennis said "It was not you that was the power of the Holy Spirit. He was slain in the Spirit and the Lord's taking care of him and working on him, pray for someone else". Well I did and boom they went down under the power of the Holy Spirit. I was so excited that night I didn't know what to do. I didn't understand it, all I knew is that it was God and to be a small part of it was just a marvelous revelation and experience for me. This is how I came to know that was what an anointing was and what God could do through a person. I prayed about the square I saw on my hands. I asked the Lord, what does that signify? In my spirit the Lord said to me . . . ." That's the nails in your hand when I was crucified. I said "but nails are round . . . that can't be it, these are square. As I related this someone spoke up and said, "In Jesus' time they did not have nails all they had were pegs of wood and they were square and that is what they nailed Him to the cross with, these square pegs. What an awesome thing that the Lord showed me that He has given me a healing ministry. There is an anointing there, when I feel the heat in my hands I know it's Jesus, not me. I know it's Him, not me, who heals. You see, there's nothing I can do to heal anybody. I'm not the healer, Jesus is the Healer through the Holy Spirit. It's an awesome thing, I know I am not worthy, but Jesus says we are worthy, as we look to Him and what He does.

There have been many funny instances of things that have happened. I remember one night some of the prayer team were praying for people in another room and Phil Valenti came out to get me, they wanted me to come in and pray and I was talking to Joe Winchell at the time and I just had a small prayer with him and as I turned around to tell

Phil I'd be right there, Joe fell face first on the floor. He dropped everything and just fell face first on the floor and I didn't know what to do, I was so upset. "Well come on in and pray" Phil said, "you have the anointing . . . he's ok, he's with the Lord". He was fine, he wasn't hurt or anything so I went and prayed with the others. Afterwards he said he was just fine and was blessed by the Lord.

Another night we were in the other room praying for people and Joe came in and wanted prayer. Joe was totally deaf. Well, anyhow, we laid hands on him and he was standing a few feet from the wall. He kind of backed up a little bit as I went to lay hands on him as he fell in the Spirit he slid down the wall and as he did, his back hit the light switch and the lights went out. God sure has a sense of humor. We stood there and laughed so hard . . . it sure was the joy of the Lord! We must have all needed it, we were laughing so hard, it was just so funny. God is funny.

Then there was the time I prayed for Sister Susan, she wanted joy. She said "I don't have much joy, I really need some joy". I said "Ok all's we have to do is ask . . . the joy of the Lord is our strength." I went to lay hands on her and I started laughing and I couldn't stop laughing. She started laughing and couldn't stop either. Someone said "You're supposed to be serious, this is serious stuff, you're supposed to be praying . . . what are you doing?" God knew what we needed before we even asked, she knew and I knew it and we couldn't stop. It really was Holy Spirit laughter and we couldn't stop. We laughed for I don't know how long. The Lord gave it to us before we even asked. What joy!

Then the time the Lord had me ask Joe if he would like prayer as He was going to lengthen his leg. Did he have one leg shorter than the other? I had never noticed it before and I was really afraid to ask Joe, but I did. I said "The Lord told me to have you sit down and for me to pray for you and He would lengthen your leg. Is one leg shorter than the other?" "Yes, it is", Joe said, "I limp all the time". I had never really noticed it. While he was sitting, we measured the two legs held them out straight and sure enough one was about 2 inches shorter than the other. Well, different people were praying and I held his leg out and as I prayed I was holding the leg out straight in my hand and I could feel and see the leg moving forward in my hand and I could feel and see the leg moving as it was lengthened by the power of Jesus Christ of Nazareth. What a joy! Joe no longer limped, he had two legs the same length. Praise the Lord! What rejoicing there was as everyone witnessed Joe walking up and down the room.

There are so many wonderful things that happened in these prayer meetings, many healings, physically, mentally and spiritual. Many who accepted the Lord into their heart and were able to grow in Him. We were taught Scripture and allowed to learn the things of God without feeling selfconscious. We were encouraged to grow in the Lord and seek the gifts and promises God has for us as we are obedient to His Word. It is for today not just for those in the Bible but for all believers. It was an experience I cherish for it has helped me to have a deeper faith and confidence in God and His Word. HE is alive! He will work in us and through us if we give Him our all and let Him. Praise the Lord!

HE IS REAL!

———————————————— ⁓⁓⁓ ————————————————

After I had accepted the Lord and was filled with the Holy Spirit with evidence of speaking in tongues I was with Joanne again, we were having lunch with Marilyn, who was a Jewish Christian. As we were eating lunch at her home, she had a couple of cats, the cats would just come and meow at me. It wasn't even a meow it was a funny sound, I can't quite describe it to you . . . but it was weird. Marilyn said well the cat is just speaking to you he wants you to play with him. So I would try to play with it and it would back away from me and hiss . . . it was almost like a growl. Anyhow, we ate lunch but I felt a little funny and did not know why I was feeling that way. It was a nice lunch and after we finished Marilyn was supposed to meet us back at Joanne's house as she had to go someplace. So, we left and as I was driving Joanne back home I said to her, "Did you feel funny while you were in there? She said "no". I said, "I just felt very cold, something very cold in there and I felt kind of funny about it." And she said "Serena I believe that is because you were discerning something, as a new child of God has very good discernment and I believe you are discerning that there is evil in her home. I said well, I really don't know. She said well, when Marilyn comes back we'll pray and you should pray because you experienced it. I said "I have never done this before and she said to just trust the Lord, He'll give you the words. When Marilyn came, I said to Joanne "I can't tell this girl

. . . I just met her . . . I can't tell her she has evil in her house". Joanne said she'll understand, she's a Christian. Probably, whatever, so she told Marilyn and Marilyn said oh, ok. Let's join hands and pray. So, I started to pray and as I prayed, my chest got heavier and heavier and heavier and I said to Joanne I can't continue to pray. My chest

34

hurts me so bad. She said Well, we have to go down there and pray against it. It is something we can't do long distance . . . . and I said I don't know anything about it and she said well come on we have to do it. I said I don't have time my kids are going to be out of school soon. Joanne said, "We have time before your kids get out of school . . . let's go!" So we went down and all the way down to Marilyn's house I did not know what to do. I said, Joanne do you know what to do? She said no, I don't. I said Great! We're two good ones, neither of us know what to do but you're telling me I have to go down and pray and get the evil out of the house and I do not know how to do it at all". So she looked up in the scriptures in Ephesians about putting on the Armor of God and said, "In the Name of Jesus you just cover us and the home with the blood of Jesus and you just pray and ask the Lord to give you discernment and show you what to do and what to say, and then you just let Him lead you. I said "Well, I don't know what I'm doing but I'll do what you said". We walked in the house and the first thing Marilyn said was, "It's not my cats." But, that cat kept growling at me. As we walked in the door the cat was sitting on the divan and I was standing there and as I was looking around our eyes locked, the cat and myself. And I was almost mesmerized by those eyes. I could see Satan in those eyes, I just knew it was him and I said "There has to be something in that cat". I had to literally take my eyes away from that cat. But, in the Name of Jesus I cast out anything that was evil in that cat and in the other cat who promptly left the room. Then we went into the room with her paintings. Marilyn was an artist and some of her works were done before she was born again and there was evil in them which was cast out. We went through all the rooms putting the blood of Jesus over them and casting out whatever came into my head. Praise the Lord the tightness in my chest left and after I had prayed for the cats they did not growl, they purred. Hallelujah! To Jesus be all the glory! He is true to His Word.

I knew that I had seen Satan. I had come face to face with him and I knew that God, through the Lord Jesus Christ had given me the power to cast him out. God had shown me through His Word, and the power of the Holy Spirit and I praise God for it! It was very, very scary but I had the assurance that God was greater than anything and that His Word is true and we can cast out evil. He has given to the church, the body of Christ, the ability and the power to do it. Weird? I'll say it was, but God turned it into a victory!

When we left Marilyn's house the first time to go to Joanne's, Marilyn had given us each some plants. We had put mine in our garage and Joanne's was in her car. When she got home she had a funny feeling as she was getting out of her car and I did in my garage and come to find out it was the plants. Apparently, some evil had attached itself we cast it out and got rid of the plants. Evil is very real but God is greater!

IT IS SO SIMPLE IT'S DIFFICULT

I know you've probably read many ways of how to give up smoking, but I don't believe you've read how this feat was accomplished in the following manner . . . .

It was terrible when I started smoking, I'd try one and cough, and say who would want to do that. Then the opportunity would come up and I'd try it again. Just one at a time. Finally, I was hooked. I smoked cigarette after cigarette until that was the first thing I did in the morning and the last thing I did at night gradually getting up to smoking over three packs a day. It got so I couldn't laugh as I would start coughing so hard I'd almost get sick. My throat and chest hurt so much afterward that I would try to avoid laughing.

My parents and others told me smoking was unlady like; that my hair and clothes smelled; my breath repulsive; but none of this deterred me. I had many allergies and had myself deluded to the fact that the allergies would be just as bad whether I smoked or not. I had given up smoking for three months and my allergies were as bad as ever so I went back to smoking and the number I had a day kept increasing. BUT I enjoyed smoking, I felt it made me relax and it was really the only thing I did. I wasn't hurting anyone, I consoled myself, and I enjoyed it. I knew in my heart it wasn't good for me, but didn't I have the right to choose what I wanted to do with my life?

A girlfriend of mine, Joanne, had an incurable back condition. She needed to wear a back brace to be able to sit, and couldn't sit very long at all . . . . as she was in constant pain. She also had a terrible burning sensation due to the damage to her nerve endings at the end of her spine. It broke my heart at times when I'd go visit her, because she'd be in such terrible pain. She'd lay flat on the floor, to get the vegetables she was going to have for supper, as she couldn't bend to the floor. She wouldn't let you do it for her, because she wanted to be able to do for herself as long as she possibly could. If she kept going, she wouldn't get completely stiff from not using her muscles. On real bad days, she couldn't pull herself back to her feet without help. On these particularly bad days that I would happen to visit her, we would pray together for relief from the pain she was experiencing. (Something I had never done before). She told me that she would then feel much better for a while.

Then one day Joanne told me she had heard about healing services that were being held near Boston, Massachusetts, and that she was planning to go. I was so pleased she was going, but a little apprehensive. Yes, I believed the Lord could do it! Butttt

. . . .

Due to the fact my part-time job was becoming a full-time one at this particular time of year, I was unable to visit Joanne for a while. I'd get out of work just in time to be home for my children when they came home from school. When she got back from Boston, she called me and very joyously told me she had been HEALED. She was no longer wearing her back brace and THE PAIN WAS GONE. As soon as I could, I just had to get over there and see her for myself. I was very excited for Joanne. I hesitate to say I didn't believe her, but I was very dubious. She was just bubbling over and I was very happy for her, but for some reason I was really bothered. There were all kinds of things that came up which made it impossible for me to stop by, have coffee and hear all about what happened to her, and then see for myself if she was healed. The day I finally was able to go to her home I was very uncomfortable. This was the first time I had ever been uncomfortable visiting my dear friend. When I arrived another lady was there. Joanne introduced us and the lady said she was just leaving but would Joanne please pray for her and her son. "Sure"! Joanne said, and she asked if I'd pray with them. I thought quickly, this was odd, but I said, "sure". We all joined hands and Joanne led the prayer. All of a sudden, she started talking funny. I had all I could do to suppress the laughter building up inside me. I reprimanded myself, thinking I shouldn't laugh, this was serious, we were praying to God!

Well, I managed to contain myself until she finished. Then I had to say, "What on earth were you doing when you were praying?" You sounded so funny, I had all I could do not to laugh. She said she didn't realize she was doing it. "Doing what?" I demanded. She kind of chuckled, and explained to me it was the gift of the Holy Spirit. She was "praying in tongues" or "praying in the Spirit". It was a gift from God. Anyone who asked for it and really desired it in their heart and stood believing would receive it from God.

Joanne asked me also if I believed in Jesus Christ, if I knew He died on the cross for my sins. I said I did. I knew He died on the cross, but never really thought about the fact that He died for my sins (personally). She told me to ask the Lord's forgiveness for my sins and invite Jesus to come into my heart and that I would be what they call "born again". Well, I was so excited, I couldn't wait to get home. When I arrived, no one was around yet . . . . Great! . . . . I ran upstairs to my bedroom and shut the door. I got down on my knees beside my bed and prayed: **Lord, please forgive me for my sins, anything I might have done that was not right in Your eyes. I am very sorry for offending You in any way. I am thankful that I now understand fully how You gave Your only Son, Jesus Christ to us, so that He would endure everything we humans would ever endure and much more, so that we could be saved and be made right with God That He was crucified and died for our sins and rose again that I may have eternal life. Yes you died, for my sins, personally. The ones I committed today and yesterday. Jesus, you went through all this just for me? Oh, Jesus how you suffered for me. Thank you, Jesus, I love you. Please come into my heart and make me be the person you want me to be. In Jesus' Name. Amen** WOW! I also asked for the gift of tongues. I did not receive it. The next day I prayed again . . . nothing. The day after that I prayed . . . . nothing. Boy, was I upset! I marched right over to Joanne's house and told her about it . . . . "I thought you said the gift of tongues was a gift from God!" All you had to do was ask for it and you would receive it! Well, I asked and asked, and I haven't received it! WHY??? She then asked me if I had ever read my horoscope or used a ouija board, had my palm read, etc. I said I had, but I didn't believe in them. "It didn't matter if you believed it or not, you, must renounce Satan, who is connected with all these things", she said. So when I went home and knelt by the bed and told the Lord Jesus I was sorry for doing these things and I ordered Satan to leave my life in the name of Jesus. Then I asked again for the gift of tongues and received it! Praise the Lord! Yes, I received the gift and prayed in the Spirit. I cried tears of joy for well over a half hour. It was so beautiful and I was so honored that the Lord chose me to have His gift. I will be forever grateful. So quickly and so simply, I was born again and filled with the Holy Spirit. How great God is!!

A few days later, I went to Joanne's home again. I told her how much I was being bugged about my smoking, and that I had tried many times to give it up and I couldn't. She said to me, "Why don't you give it up to the Lord? "Have Him take care of it". So, I did pray about it, I asked, "Lord, only You can deliver me from smoking . . . I've tried to stop and I can't . . . I can't do it myself . . . I need Your help . . . please help me . . . take away my desire to smoke . . . . In Jesus' Name." I waited . . . . nothing happened . . . . so I waited some more and knew it would happen in His time not mine. So I waited and was still smoking away . . . . People kept asking me why I don't give up the cigarettes. I just kept saying I had given it over to the Lord; when He wanted me to stop, He would take away my desire. Finally, my husband said, "You've got to help yourself!" So, I threw my cigarettes in the trash. In a few hours, which seemed like days, I went back and dug out the cigarettes, and started smoking again.

One month from the time I gave it to the Lord, I woke up and had a cigarette, which tasted horrible. I knew this time God was working. This time I had a whole carton in my kitchen cabinet and threw them all in the trash. I have not had the desire for a cigarette since that day in 1980. I am also thrilled about one very significant thing. That is, I can laugh again. I can just let loose and there's no coughing. I can really laugh freely without the dread of ending up choking and hurting. What a joy that is! Joanne says when we get to heaven, she'll know me right away, by my laugh.

I thank and praise the Lord Jesus Christ for this miracle in my life. I didn't give up the cigarettes by myself, but by the grace of God . . . . He took my desire away. I don't even desire one to this day like so many do that give it up on their own. They still have the desire. I thank God for helping me and I give Him all the glory . . . it is through Him and by Him I no longer smoke. If He can do it for me He can do it for you. Whatever it is that has you in its clutches give it to God and let Him help you.

It is so simple to look to the Lord. It is so simple to accept Jesus into your heart . . . . to be "born again". It is so simple to give all of your worries and cares to the Lord Jesus and let Him take care of them. I'm not suggesting you sit back and do nothing. I am saying, bring it to the Lord. Ask His help and guidance . . . He wants us to do this. And He's always there ready with His love overflowing for us, ready to help in any way. He wants us to do this but . . . . it is so simple, it is difficult for most of us to believe it. Well, I am living proof, I've been there, believe it! Then, you too can find peace and joy in your life that only God can give through trusting Christ Jesus.

If you desire a personal relationship with the Lord Jesus Christ repeat the prayer I had prayed or something similar in your own words, God knows your heart . . . . and you too will be "born again" and will be a child of the King. "For unless ye be born again ye cannot enter the Kingdom of God".

If you have any questions or if you have accepted Jesus through this testimony please E-mail me, at smjpray@aol.com, so that I may rejoice with you.

GOD'S WRITING ON MY HAND

On Friday, September 5th, 1980 the most amazing thing happened!!!!
I was led of the Lord to go over to Joanne Rosney's and tell her that
the Lord wanted us to sit and talk—just the two of us and to take the
phone off the hook and not to be disturbed—if we had to go out, we'd
go out, but otherwise take the phone off the hook so we wouldn't be
disturbed and the two of us had to just be together . . . . alone . . . and
just PRAISE THE LORD!

We were going to have lunch and because Joanne had been on the
phone all morning she hadn't had a chance to get dressed yet, so while
she was dressing, I made lunch. As we sat to eat we said grace. When
finished, I said to Joanne—"Gee, my hands are burning terrible" and
she came and looked at my hands and there was writing on my left
hand. It looked like blue pen. You couldn't really make out the writing
and there was two lines of it. Joanne said, "That is of the Lord!" "No,"
I said, "I must have put my hand on something and the writing came
off." As I checked everything I had touched and saw nothing that could
come off she said, "No, no, no, that is of the Lord! Let's see what it
says . . . . I think we'll have to use a mirror to read it". We went into
the bathroom and held up my hand and sure enough, the writing was
more distinct. Joanne said, "It says CHRIST I AM on the top." At first
I couldn't see it . . . I was kind of dubious about the whole thing . . . .
I couldn't believe it!!!! I could not fathom how it got here. So many
things were running through my mind I could not really concentrate
on it but as she pointed it out to me in the mirror I finally saw it and
almost fell over.

We stood there trying to figure out what the second line said when
Joanne exclaimed "Let's call . . . ." and I was thinking at the same time

that we should call . . ."Phil Valenti". So we dialed his number, told him a bit about what had happened and he came right over and immediately saw the CHRIST I AM also. We were all trying to figure out the rest and could not, so we prayed and asked the Lord for discernment. All of a sudden, out of the clear blue sky, I got the word SOJOURN and I knew that wasn't from me because I wouldn't use that word. I figured it was some kind of a journey or a trip or something, but wasn't sure the exact meaning. We all looked and that is exactly what we saw . . . SOJOURN!

Finally, I had to leave as my children were due home from school. It was really exciting to see the writing in the mirror like it was written inside of me. Mind boggling!! I tried to figure out what it meant so I looked up Christ in the back of my bible and it said THE ANOINTED ONE . . . . THE ANOINTED ONE, I AM! Then I looked up SOJOURN and it said . . . ."You're there for a little while . . . you'd just be there for a while." Later, as I was talking to Kay Winchell and she told her husband Joe about what happened, he said, "Oh yes . . . that definitely is of God". I asked her how he knew and she said he had this book that he had read and this has happened to several people. But what it is saying is that Jesus was in me for a little while and then I knew . . . you know how something hits you and you just know it's the truth! What an awesome thing to think of, just beautiful . . . I couldn't help it but tears just came. Oh, what a humbling experience! God is so good! I know that I know that I know that He was definitely in me. Where the two words started there was two veins and it was like it was written in blood. It was just . . . I can't explain it to you . . . but it was just beautiful! The Jesus within me talked to me through the writing on my hand to let me know that He's there! I just praise God for that and also that His anointing was there with the burning of my hands . . . I felt it, I knew it, I saw it! HALLELUJAH!!!

KEEPER OF THE WELL

After praying awhile, I thought, I've done a lot of talking, maybe I ought to listen for awhile. So, I said "OK, Lord, what do you have to say to me? I am listening". While waiting, I began to see in my mind's eye, Jesus sitting at a well. You know, an old fashioned one with a bucket. "Come to Me, all who are weary and heavy laden and I shall give thee rest", He seemed to be saying. Just as He is the Shepherd of the sheep . . . He is Keeper of the well. He wants us to come to Him with our burdens and cares and willfully give them to Him as He waits by the well. Close your eyes . . . can you see Him? As you talk to Him and give Him the problem, disease, hurt, anxiety, anger, loneliness, or whatever is bothering you whether it was in the past or is happening right now. Then picture yourself giving it to Jesus and watch Him as He throws it in this bottomless well so that we are set free. This is just like when we go to Him and ask forgiveness for our sin and He throws it as far as the East is to the West never to be remembered. There is also living water in the well, and when Jesus throws that problem in . . . . Listen . . . . for the splash . . . and feel it as the power of the Holy Spirit is released and washes over your body and mind to give you that peace, healing and release, as the grime, dirt, heaviness, guilt, disease, anger and/or sorrow, is removed by God's pure love for you through Jesus. Our hope, peace and joy is renewed when we again realize, when we let go and let God . . . . ALL things are possible.

Will you meet Jesus at the well? Think on these things. You'll be glad you did!

SOARING ON BROKEN WINGS

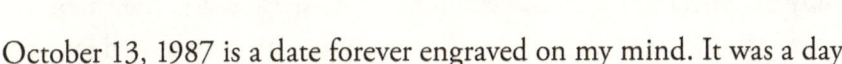

October 13, 1987 is a date forever engraved on my mind. It was a day that was to drastically change my life.

With my children grown, I was working as a Secretary/Receptionist for an auditing firm. This particular day, as my boss was squatting in front of the mail table, he asked me if we needed to order more padded envelopes. I got up from my desk and walked over to the mail table and as I bent down to look, I had to twist my body somewhat to see past him. As I did so, a sharp pain went down my lower back and into my left leg. I said Oh and straightened up and then did the same thing again trying to see and this time the pain was unbearable so I sat down. Within five minutes I couldn't sit or stand on my left leg due to severe pain. The ambulance crew that had to be summoned, carried me from our office and then transported me and my boss, to the hospital. My husband had been called at work and was to meet us there. After almost nine hours in the hall of the emergency room, I was examined and taken to Xray. The diagnosis was spondylosis and a herniated disc in the lower lumbar region. Due to the fact that there was no room for me in the hospital, I was sent home, after receiving a shot and some pills for the pain. It was tough for Don as I screamed in pain all the way home from having to sit in the car.

For three and a half weeks I was at home on my couch with a board under the cushions and a commode next to me. I was supposed to be on complete bed rest but had to go to see the doctors, several in fact. The neurologist I was sent to could not do a test with needles that the doctor had ordered, due to the extreme pain and sensitivity in my leg. She was afraid the needles would break off in my leg and then I'd be in more trouble. I had sciatica in the left leg and couldn't stand anything even brushing against it, let alone a sheet or something lying on it.

All during this time period, I was unable to sleep because of the constant pain. Many medications were tried but I had some kind of adverse reaction to all of them. Most made me like a zombie, but I couldn't sleep, and they didn't dull the pain. While on yet another medication, with no relief, I was terribly distraught, depressed and desperate for some relief. After three and a half weeks of agony and no sleep, I tried to crawl upstairs, to get dressed, so I could go out into the middle of the street and get hit by a car. My husband and children were so upset they left one daughter with me and drove to the doctor's office and insisted I be admitted to a hospital where I could be properly cared for and they could see what wasn't helping. This was late in the evening, and I had calmed down a bit by the time they got back so I agreed to wait until morning. The next morning, I was brought by ambulance to a different hospital where I was kept for twelve days. While there they started me on Physical Therapy. When I was discharged I could walk with the aid of a walker and was told to continue with physical therapy three times a week.

Within a few weeks, the muscles in my neck and shoulders and upper back would spasm and be very sore and painful. Because of these symptoms, the inability to sleep, and her examination, my regular doctor suspected that as a complication of the original injury, I had developed Fibrositis, which at that time was not very well understood. So she, in turn, made an appointment with an Arthritis Doctor for me and provided him with my background. After his complete examination and the testing of what the medical community calls "Trigger Points", he confirmed the diagnosis of Fibrositis.

With this being a Worker's Compensation case I was advised to get an additional opinion. My doctor referred me to a Rheumatologist and also provided him with my background. Upon completion of his examination, he told me that due to the injury and the resultant constant pain with no sleep the Fibrositis had been triggered. He also said that an injury induced case of Fibrositis was usually worse than for someone who developed it slowly through the years. Fibrositis is also called Fibromyalgia and linked with Chronic Fatigue Syndrome, among others. It is called a "functional disease" where the function of the organ changes from the way it should work. Prolonged dysfunction can cause tissue damage. It is a Rheumatic disease frequently involving muscles, tendons, ligaments, skin, fascia (connective tissue covering or binding together body structures) and bones. The predominant symptom is pain. He explained it was not life-threatening but that I fell into the advanced category with multiple symptoms and in my particular case it was irreversible. There is no cure. With the inability to sleep properly (I don't sleep deep enough for my muscles to automatically relax), there is constant pain and fatigue. He also said to get a lot of rest, try to walk three times a week with a goal of 2 miles each time and to Think Positive and Don't Give Up! Stress and weather changes worsen the pain and many times restrict mobility. I should do stretching exercises in order to keep mobility. I was to avoid stress, not to get excited "good" or "bad". Do what I can and what will not cause me extra, lasting pain.

One of the biggest frustrations of this disease is that it is not something you can see. You look like you are in perfect health. You don't "look sick"! many persons have called me a hypochondriac or lazy or have said to me "its all in your mind", mostly during the Worker's Compensation hearings, but also some of the doctors I've seen over the years. It is a constant struggle to keep a positive outlook.

My lawyer is still shaking his head at what the Lord accomplished at my last hearing. It had been a three year battle and each hearing made me physically worse from the stress. At this particular hearing the insurance company lawyer told the Judge "If you rule for them I'll appeal and if you rule for us they'll appeal . . . . One way or another your decision will be appealed"! The Judge looked at me and said "you win"! I looked at him and said "What"? He said "You win, I'm ruling in your favor". Astonished and at a loss for words, I just said "Thank you, Sir"! He then said "That's it, it's all over, you can go". My lawyer was surprised also but he said "Well, just remember they are definitely going to appeal so expect to hear from them". He marked my file "Will Definitely Appeal". I put the entire situation in God's hands that day and Praise the Lord! They DID NOT APPEAL! Finally, after three years of hearings, doctors, etc., I was found to be

75% Permanently Disabled by the Worker's Compensation Board and Judge.

My life, before this incident, was very full. A wife, mother of three, took care of our home, inside and out, worked outside the home to help with college expenses, was very active in church, including doing the newsletters and served on various committees, etc. I enjoyed bowling and recently had taken up golf.

Today, my life is limited, as most of the time I have to push myself to do things, as I am tired and hurting all of the time. My husband helps me by vacuuming, washing and waxing floors. He also does my windows and mirrors for if I exert pressure on my hands to scrub, rub or try to open jars a shooting pain goes up my arm into my shoulder. If I stand very long in one place I experience pain in my back. I also cannot sit too long at one time. If I try to type I can only do a little at a time as it causes muscle spasms and pain. It has taken me two days to type this. I can no longer bowl or golf but I still dabble a bit in writing.

As you can see, it is a day to day struggle, but I'm not alone. I have my family and friends who care and try to understand. They pray for me constantly. I also know that God is always there and that He understands. They say there's no cure but you can feel better if you are allowed to go at your own pace because only you know how you feel and what sets your muscles or body off to more pain. As of this writing I am off all medication, have lost some weight and am exercising on a stationery bicycle and walking when weather permits. This has helped some with sleeping. I still hurt every day and when the weather changes it is a lot worse and there are days that I still get frustrated and depressed. There are also some days that I feel good, comparatively. Somehow, with God's help, most days I am able to soar above it and take one day at a time.

"But those who hope in the Lord will renew their strength.
They will soar on wings like eagles; they
will run and not grow weary,
they will walk and not be faint."
Isaiah 40:31 NIV

MACULAR DEGENERATION

We got to Florida late in January 2004 because my eye had been bleeding and I finally had to have laser surgery to stop the leak (wet macular degeneration). I got permission to have it checked with a retina specialist while down there. We were in Florida only three days when my husband's sister went to be with the Lord, so we took the train back to Rhode Island for the funeral as we were both wiped out from driving down (took us 4 days as we stopped one night at my sister's in Titusville). We stayed with our daughter and son in law and our 3 grandchildren for a few days and took train back to Pinellas Park to our son's after the funeral.

After we returned to Florida I noticed more of my sight was going but thought it was scar tissue forming and waited for two weeks until my scheduled appointment with the eye doctor to have it checked. He said my eye was leaking (bleeding) again but this time in the center where if I had laser again would be a definite blind spot. He said I needed either the cold laser which would involve putting dye in my arm and laser treatment about $1500 each time 4 or 5 times and afterward had to be covered head to toe so sunlight would not touch my skin because dye would make me photosensitive . . . . OR, I could have surgery where they put a hole in my eye and take out the abnormal blood vessels and then I would have to bend over all the time for a while or something like that . . . . He said to make up my mind quickly and do something right away and that he did one thing Thursday's and another on Saturday's . . . . this was on a Monday. My spirit said NO . . . I told him I will go back up north to do anything in my familiar surroundings and in my own home. We immediately packed and started back up north the following day. We got home on

Friday night and called our Pastor and told him what the Lord laid upon my heart to be anointed with oil and prayed for by the elders of the church. I also asked prayer for a revitilization of the Healing Ministry the Lord had given me. So they prayed . . . when we were driving home from church I said to my hubby (Don) I can see through the grey spot. All this is in my left eye and this leak was a big grey spot right in the middle of my vision . . . like putting a dime over a picture right in the middle it blocks out everything there you can see the stuff around that circle but not straight on. Anyway was like seeing a negative after the prayer black and white and not too clear but the grey was gone . . . still see a circle around it but could see stuff . . . all I could think of was Bartimeus and how when the Lord touched his eyes at first he could see people like trees . . . Well went to my doctor in Troy on Monday and he said the bleeding had stopped . . . . I said Praise the Lord! and told him about the Pastor and elders anointing and praying for me. He said we'll take all the help we can get. He told me that the cold laser and the operation because of where it is . . . the risks out weigh the benefits and he would not suggest it. I said Praise the Lord! I had asked him before we left for Florida if he had ever seen a miracle . . . that I believe God can perform miracles even if he did the laser which he did before we left in January on the other spot in that eye. So he said to me we will wait and see . . . we'll keep an eye on it to see what happens . . . . but his idea of a miracle is for God to reverse the process. I said God can do that too! He made another appointment for the next week. I had the Pastor and elders pray again last Sunday and went Tuesday this week and he said it is healing and forming a scab by itself . . . Ha ha.(by GOD) but was still a bit swollen and it is his hope that it will continue to heal and I should regain some sight . . . He said no lifting, no bending, no stress . . . . and keep up the prayers . . . . come back in two weeks. So have an appointment on the 30th of March.

Update: Never had to have a laser treatment or surgery . . . Praise the Lord! I am so excited about what the Lord is doing! To God be the glory!!!!!! As of September 2007 I have still got the grey area in the middle of the left eye but have not had any more bleeding and the right eye which has this also is clear and no bleeding . . . . Praise the Lord, He has stopped any further deterioration of the eyes and I am just waiting on the Lord with anticipation for my complete healing and the healing of others!

God's Word is TRUE!

THE BIOPSY

On September 8th, 2005 went for my yearly mammogram. On Monday the 12th they called and said I needed to come back for a few more films on my left breast. They scheduled me for the 21st. I went back and they took a few more pictures then had me wait . . . they came back and said they wanted to do an ultra sound as something showed up on the pictures and they wanted to check it out. They could do it right away, the Doctor would do it herself, so I would know right away. So they did the ultra sound. When she finished she said she did not like the looks of it and wanted to do a biopsy. It was new from last year and about ½ inch at widest point. It was not a cyst. It was elongated with little branches sticking out. I asked if she could explain to both of us and I went out to get Don in the waiting room. When we came back she explained to us that she was not going to pull any punches, she knew it was a shock, but if it was cancer, it was in a good place and it was small. All that would have to be done would be to make an incision and scoop the tumor out and after 6 weeks have 6 weeks of radiation.

Prognosis: Excellent . . . then go on with my life. The first step is the biopsy then a surgeon . . . whatever the biopsy showed would determine the treatment.

Being a woman of faith I put my name on the prayer networks that I am involved in and told them about the biopsy and that I was going to a Woman of Faith conference on the 23rd and 24th and on Sunday the 25th I asked my Pastor if he would anoint me with oil and have the elders pray over me as James 5:13 says to do in the Bible.

During the Conference on Friday night Patsy Clairmont was ministering and she hysterically explained how when she did not submit to authority what happened . . . . when she did not listen to her husband . . . . it was so funny but true when we think we know best. How God tells us things or warns us in His Word and we think oh we can do that . . . it was a great conference and we got home late and I was way overtired . . . we were supposed to meet at 7:45 in the morning and I did not sleep until about 3:30 or 4AM and was up about 5:30AM. I have Fibromyalgia and my muscles were hurting and I just could not go . . . so I called and told them and rested on Saturday.

Saturday night I went to bed at 8PM fell asleep right away and woke up about 10PM, went back to sleep and about midnight our upstairs neighbor got home and opened the sliding door to their porch which woke both of us up and she was banging around up there. I was not a happy camper, but finally fell back to sleep. Woke up about 5AM and was talking to the Lord in my head as I was thinking about my going up for prayer and I thought of the verse, "When you go to the altar if you have ought against your brother leave the altar and go and reconcile then come back and pray".

I said "Lord if I have anything against anyone show me so that I will be right with you when I am being prayed for and also the people who are praying for me." Then, James 5:13 came to mind, "Confess your sin one to another that you may be healed". "Well Lord, I can't think of anything off hand, would it be someone who is going to pray for me?" Then at breakfast I said to Don "Did you hear her last night! Woke me right up and he said, "me too." It was then it hit me . . . . God was trying to tell me, and I wasn't listening. Finally it dawned on me, I was really annoyed with my neighbor for being so noisy so late at night, I had to forgive her. So I prayed and asked forgiveness of the Lord for being so upset and that I chose to forgive her, would He help? Well I realized she probably doesn't know how much noise she makes, as no one has ever told her, but it was ok. The Lord gave me such a peace. But all I could think of was the story Patsy Clairmont told us at the conference and how I knew what I was doing but I wasn't really listening. When I submitted to God's way, He gave me peace and I was able to go to the altar in accordance with the Word of God. To God be the glory!

I was excited to see what would happen the next day in light of being obedient to His Word, being anointed and having the elders pray for healing and a good report after confessing my sin to the Lord and forgiving my neighbor.

Well, I had the biopsy. You talk about fear and trepidation! My blood pressure before the procedure was 199/108 . . . talk about anxiety! They were very sweet and told me exactly what was going to happen . . . . it burned a bit when they put the needle in but after that I could feel nothing and they talked with me while she was looking at the ultrasound to get it into position. Then they told me it would sound like a staple gun when she took a piece and it did . . .but did not bother me. She took 3 biopsies, they cleaned up the area, put steri strips on where she went in and said that is it! Praise the Lord for the prayers! It really was not bad, I have been through worse with a root canal. I did have a boo boo boobie for a day or so and was a bit sore but not bad. I took tylenol and that helped. So for anyone facing that procedure, it really is not bad, the worst part of the whole thing is waiting. Thank God I did not have to wait a long time for the biopsy but the time I waited before going in was awful. We were told to come early and we did, and then they were late taking me in because of a conference, so I was pretty nervous by then. Had the biopsy Monday the 26th and then an appointment for the surgeon on Wednesday the 28th and we were hoping the biopsy would be back.

On Tuesday, the 27th, I had an appointment with the ophthalmologist regarding the macular degeneration. I asked the Lord if somehow he would give me a word through the doctor. I had to have dye put in my arm for pictures so I asked them to check with the doctor if it was ok, because I had the biopsy the day before. He said it was ok and I had that done. I told him what was going on and he said he was sorry to hear I was going through this and explained to me the results of the tests they had taken on my eyes. He said you have a real good report . . . I was worried about your right eye . . . but it is just perfect no sign of bleeding etc. and the left eye, other than the blind spot from before, was perfectly healthy also. Praise the Lord! Then he shocked me . . . he said I want to tell you something, my wife had breast cancer, she had it all over her body and had surgery, radiation, chemo and stem cell replacement and she is fine. "Go, do what they tell you and you will be fine!" he said . . . . There was my word.

We went to see the surgeon, still no results yet for the biopsy; however, the doctor showed us all the x-rays and ultra sound pictures etc. I had to fill out a mountain of paper work, the way back medical history stuff . . . I cheated and brought papers with dates etc . . . good thing I never could have remembered it all and it still took me about 40 minutes to make them out between them taking my blood pressure etc. The Doctor talked with both Don and I and then sent him out while she examined me. When she finished they brought Don back in and told us I was at low risk for breast cancer but that did not mean I did not have it. She also asked me if I had ever been in an accident and I told her no, which I hadn't but remembered afterward we had been in an almost accident where we had to stop fast which I called in to report on Thursday Thursday evening about 7 PM we got the call . . . . it was breast cancer . . . she wanted to see us Friday morning.

Friday morning, after not sleeping much and being in such pain with the Fibromyalgia, went to the surgeon's office and she explained it was a T 1 which was duct cancer which had broken through but only ½ inch. It probably was not in the lymph nodes but they would check that during the surgery, which still will be a lumpectomy. She scheduled the surgery for Friday, Oct. 7th at Albany Memorial Hospital and follow up to be Oct. 14th along with the Oncologist appointment the same day. They will do another biopsy first putting a wire in to guide the surgeon then bring me in to the operating room and do the lumpectomy and biopsies of the sentinel lymph nodes . . . then that will determine treatment . . . should go home same day Monday morning after a few days of pain from the Fibromyalgia it is starting to subside some . . . Was blessed by a visit from our Pastor's wife and her sister, they brought me a book written by one of the speakers at the Women of Faith Conference and prayed with me, it meant a great deal to feel so loved. Then just before noon the surgeon's office called to tell me my Pre-admission tests were tomorrow at 1:15 PM. I hung up the phone and about 5 minutes later she called again and said I had to be in the hospital Friday at 8:15 AM to do some other things before the operation. Looks like Friday is going to be a LONG day. Wish I was going to be knocked out for all of it. Not that fortunate I'm afraid, oh well, this too shall pass.

10/4 the date of the pre admission stuff . . . . arrived about 1 for a 1:15 PM appointment . . . went to the ambulatory care unit and they gave me more paper work to fill out . . . A whole new history which I did not think I had to do as the surgeon said she would fax all the stuff over . . . well she did but I still had to fill it out and sign papers . . . then the nurse brought me into a room and took my blood pressure. Their machine was not working right she said, but finally got a 176/86 with respiration 105. Was I nervous . . . . you betcha! She wanted to go through my allergies etc . . . . that is in itself something else . . . . she said I will be writing all day to put this all down. I gave her a sheet of the allergies I have and what I take for vitamins. Then she said I had to have an EKG and blood work, so Don went out to the waiting room and they did that and the allergies came into play again about the antibiotic they would use. I told the nurse the surgeon had already figured that out and it began with a G she mentioned a name and I thought that was it but was not positive, so she called the surgeon for confirmation. After the other girl drew the blood I was done . . . they gave me a sheet of what to do before surgery and what to not wear etc and then we left to go shopping. I had to get some kind of a button down shirt to wear after the surgery, so we picked one up which had snaps which was even better. I also purchased a front hook bra which I thought might be easier. Then we went out to eat . . . . and relaxed a little bit and stopped at CVS to get an ice bag for after surgery.

Wednesday . . . this is getting to be quite the adventure . . . today I got a call from the Nuclear Department saying I had to come in at 7:30 AM no matter what any one else says. I am to first go to the OR and they will give me my beautiful gown etc then they will bring me down to Nuclear Dept about 8:15-8:30 where they will put the radioactive stuff and dye in my breast . . . . she asked if I knew what they were going to do and I said put the stuff in my breast and I asked if they were going to numb it first and they said no they can't it will interfere with what they want to do, they will put 4 needles in my nipple at 12 o'clock 3,

6 & 9. They will finish with me about 9:45 AM when they will bring me to mammography to do the biopsy and wire to map what is needed to be taken, then they will bring me to the OR to be operated on at a specific time which I will know Thursday night.

Wonderful! About an hour later I receive a call from the surgeon's office that the hospital called and I need to get an exam from my regular doctor that will ok me for surgery as my EKG was different from the last one they had. Wonderful! So the woman called and got me an appointment with a different doctor but an appointment none the less to clear me for surgery. So tomorrow the day before surgery at 11:45AM I go for an exam. Meanwhile all this is really not helping the body with the Fibromyalgia. Praise the Lord! I sure will be happy when this is over the stress of everything is unbelievable! Thank God I have the Lord.

Thursday went to the doctor's office and they questioned me as to what I wanted done today and I said cleared for surgery, as the hospital found my EKG different. The doctor asked me if they faxed the EKG or what. Told them I had no idea the surgeon's office called and told me I had to have the exam and they made the appointment. So they were going to call the hospital and I said I thought you would just do another EKG. So he said yes after checking me over, etc, that would be easier . . . so they did another EKG and then he consulted with other doctors and determined I was cleared for surgery . . . the difference was a small part and not anything serious that it was ok to have surgery but I should have a stress test done after surgery from a cardiologist just so they know all is ok. He would put a referral in and I would call to make an appointment once I was feeling better. My blood pressure was 153/92 and respiration was 103. Talk about a little more stress.

Friday the day of surgery was up at 5:30AM after maybe 2 hours sleep all together. Had no breakfast as I had to fast from midnight but had nothing to eat or drink since 9:30 last night. Jodi drove us to the hospital and we arrived a little after 7 am. We checked in at the desk and they gave me my new bracelet with name, etc . . .then another bracelet with all my allergies and sent us up to OR. We checked in there and waited until about quarter to eight when they called me in and gave me a gown to wear that was very small and I asked the nurse if they had a larger one and she was so nice and got me a larger one that I could at least tie. They took blood pressure and respiration was 88 a lot better than the day before. They asked me questions and told me they would put in the IV line after all my other stuff was done, which I was very happy about. Then they allowed Don to come in and visit with me until they were going to take me downstairs to nuclear medicine. They would not let Jodi come in . . . only one at a time. She came in later and then they let me rest till they took me down to ultrasound to find the tumor again and take pictures. The Dr. of radiology, Dr. Cush came in and said he would do the injections of the nuclear stuff and blue dye right there and it was very painful but they had to do it without medication for it to work properly. He had to stick 4 needles of stuff into my nipple. One at 12 o'clock, one at 3 o'clock, one at 6 o'clock and one at 9 o'clock and it would be real painful but last only about 5 minutes and if I wanted a break in between to let him know. So I just told him to go ahead and get it over with. So he started and it was excruciating and I said "ow, ow, ow", but it would let up after a minute or so. He did two and asked if I wanted a break and I said "NO. Get it over with". The third one was not quite as bad but the fourth was a doozy. They were going to get me up and wheel me back to OR to perculate for an hour and a half but let me rest there for about 10 minutes before they moved me. They were very gentle and very compassionate. The doctor said I did real well as most people scream at the top of their lungs during the whole procedure. I did not feel like I did well but I sure was glad that part was over. They got me back to OR and let Don come in and then Jodi came in and then they let me rest . . . I was tired from the traumatic ordeal I had just been through. After about an hour and a half they came back to get me and brought me down to the nuclear medicine place where they took photographs of where the radioactive stuff went to first, which is called the sentinel node in my lymph system closest to the tumor. It took a while for each photo and I was very uncomfortable with the Fibromyalgia but they were very gentle and caring and helped me through even with the girl holding my arm up for me. When they finished they wheeled me back to ultrasound and both rooms were occupied. I was chilled so they got some warm blankets and put them around my shoulders and on my lap and I spent about a half hour in the hall waiting till they were ready for me. The next procedure was to place a wire around the tumor so the surgeon would know where to cut. I thought they were going to freeze the breast for this but the doctor said no . . . he could but would mean more needles and it was nothing like the other ones so I said ok go ahead get it over with. So he did put the needle in and played a bit with the ultrasound to guide it here and there and when he finished I had a needle and wires sticking out of my breast. They put a kind of dressing over it to cover it up until surgery and then brought me back to OR. They let Don come back in and then the Anesthesiologist came in and talked to me . . . Don went out for a few minutes and they put the IV line in. I did not want it in my hand so she put it in the elbow part as she said that would be less painful . . . she was right and did real good work, I hardly felt it. Jodi came in for a minute and then Don came back and Dr.Youngelman arrived and she said she would talk to us when she got changed and the operating room nurse was asking me questions and then said we'll see her in the operating room and I said goodbye to Don and we went to the operating room where I met Dr. Charles from anesthesia and they switched me from the stretcher and had me move to operating table. Dr. Youngelman came in and asked how I was doing and I told her I was scared to death . . . she held my hand and said it was going to be ok. I asked her if she would just put me out and Dr. Charles said I am putting some medicine in, you will feel sleepy in a minute. I said don't feel it then I said now I am feeling weird, yes really weird and that is last I remember till I came to in the recovery room. The nurse wanted to give me morphine for the pain and I did not really want it, but she insisted I needed something, so I told her ok just a little and she gave me some crackers so I could take a pill . . . she broke it in half so I could take it then afterward sat me up in a chair and finally brought me back to the original waiting place in OR and let Don and Jodi come in and we talked for a while and then they said I could go home. Jodi helped me dress and they wheeled me to the door and it was just raining a bit and Jodi drove us home. We arrived home about 5 PM all totally exhausted, it had been a long day. Cindy had arrived from Franklin and was working on our supper which sounded good as I had had nothing but a few crackers and a little bit of water all day.

I rested and took the pills every 4 hours the doctor had prescribed as I was really sore. Cindy stayed until Sunday and was very helpful in getting meals etc. which was a big blessing to both Don & I. Each day got a bit better, after about 3 or 4 days I got off the prescription medication and started taking just tylenol.

On the 12th of October I had an appointment to meet Dr. Arun Puranik, the Radiation Therapy Specialist. He discussed with us about radiation therapy and made an appointment to be mapped and measured for this while doing a CT Scan. On the 14th I had an appointment to meet the Medical Oncologist, Doctor Regina Resta and she discussed hormone therapy etc. That same afternoon I had a follow up visit with the surgeon and she said I was doing very well. They had got it all and there was no cancer found around the perimeter of the tumor or in the lymph nodes. That it was smaller than they had anticipated, less than half a centimeter. Prognosis was good. On the 25th I had the CT Scan and mapping done. It was kind of scary not knowing what they were going to do but between the prayers and my keeping my mind on Jesus I got through it fine. I have three tatoos and marks all over x's . . . . looks cute! Now they have to go through and map some more for the depth and strength of the radiation etc. when they finish in about a week or so, then I will go in for a simulation which they line you up in the machine and check to see all is ok and adjust any glitches. When all is ready then I make appointments for the actual radiation to be done. It should be approximately 30 treatments 5 a week. During the last week they give a heavier dose just where they took out the tumor. So I have a little respite as my surgery is not quite healed enough still has some scabs. So now it is wait and heal. The Lord definitely got me through today as this machine was quite close to my head and I just kept my eyes closed and kept saying Jesus help me . . . give me peace and He got me through. I was supposed to stay very still in the same position while the radiologist took some readings. Just before they finished, I asked if I could move my leg as the muscles were so tight, I tried to relax and lean it on the brace they put under my legs and my whole body was shaking . . . I told the radiologist, "I can't help it my whole body is shaking," and he put his hand on my arm and said to the girl, "she really is shaking but it doesn't show up so it's ok." Praise the Lord!

I was sure happy to get out of there. Thank God for the Lord and for the precious people praying for me. I don't know what I'd do without them. This too has passed . . . . One day at a time!

I then had almost two weeks to wait before the dry run for the radiation treatment which was on the 7th of November . . . it was kind of scary too, but everyone was so nice and Julie, the technician explained all that she was doing and going to do. On the 8th of November I had my first treatment and that was kind of scary too . . . . was it going to hurt? Was it going to take long? On and on were the questions in my mind. But Praise the Lord! I got through it and am putting Aquaphor a healing ointment on the radiated area to keep it moist and it is helping to soften the scabs I have over the incision and I wash it off with body wash at night and just wash with water in the morning before the treatment. After the treatments I go home and put the ointment on again until I go to bed when I wash it off. That first day, all I could think of was the bottle of beer on the wall song . . . I was told there would be 28 treatments . . . 28 radiation treatments to go, 28 to go, After I finish the treatment today. 27 treatments to go Hurray! As of this writing I have only 24 to go.

God never ceases to amaze me. Today after my radiation treatment as I was changing into my clothes I noticed a rash all over my upper torso and arms so I put a gown back on and asked one of the technicians if someone could look at it to see if it was from the radiation or what as I would not be back in until Monday . . . He told me to go into the first examination room and he would have the doctor come in and check me. The head radiation doctor came in and checked me and said it was just from the cold weather, no problem. Then the doctor said to me, "I took my wife in for surgery on her eye yesterday and I was reading this book while waiting for her by Serena Johnson, of course I do not know who this Serena Johnson is" and I said, "It is me." He said, "You wrote the book? I said, "yes I did." He said, "I really liked your poems, it really is you" and I said, "yes, thank you", I did not know what else to say. When my husband had his cataract surgery, the Lord prompted me to leave one of my books in the waiting room. As some of you know, it is all about Jesus and experiences I've had through the years and poems I had written, along with words from the Lord. I wondered what would happen by leaving it there. Well, today I found out that some people were reading it thanks to the Doctor telling me he had read it while waiting for his wife in surgery. God is so good . . . . Sometimes we hesitate to be obedient and miss God. I was so happy I listened . . . . To God be the glory! That was very precious to me to know someone was reading the book and enjoyed it.

It was good to have the weekend off and now we begin again tomorrow. Friday Don had a 101 fever and took 2 tylenol then still took me to my treatment . . . I got in there and they had me all set up to start and the machine froze . . . like a computer software . . . . they had to get me back up and restart the whole machine again then get me all set up again . . . crazy but I finally got the treatment and poor Don had to wait extra and not feeling good . . . . tonite the fever came back so he needs prayer . . . Thank God for the weekend we both need the rest and only 3 days next week then 4 days off . . . I am so tired . . . between the fibromaylgia and the treatments and everything going on, I am just weary. When we are weak, He is strong Amen? Don still has fever today. Saturday, we wanted to go to the luncheon today at church but cannot hopefully, this fever will go soon, he does not have really any other symptoms except feeling weak. He feels better with tylenol, I'm just asking the Lord to heal him, to set him free from whatever it is.

Went to cardiologist the 28th of November and she said looking at my different EKG's I had, they are all the same . . . . they are normal for me . . . they did an ultra sound in middle of my chest with no leads to check and see if I had a heart attack previous and all was ok,.no problem she said. "get the radiation done, go to Florida and when I get back she will do a work up and check me all out but all looks good to her." A note about the fibromyalgia, while doing the ultra sound they had me hold my breath and I got a spasm in my back and I said "ow" and moved and the doctor said, "look at that, its moving I can see the spasm . . . look at it move." I provided entertainment for them anyway.

Praise the Lord! Yesterday, I found out all my tests were ok. The bone scan showed no cancer but some arthritis in my spine, knees and ankles. The liver ultrasound showed no cancer but have fatty liver, with no gall bladder it is ok I guess. Chest x rays were fine the pancreas they could not see, the kidneys were clear so Praise the Lord, all good reports! Had a good thing happen today found out my last radiation will be Dec. 23rd . . . . now I have something to look forward to. Praise the Lord! Having some burning and itching from radiation and the fibromyalgia is not great with the cold, but this too shall pass. The Lord is covering me with His wings.

Don found out he has to have a laser treatment on the eye he has been having trouble with on Jan 5th. There is a very thin membrane left from cataract surgery that should correct the rest in his eye. The swelling has gone down and no more drops, thank God. So things are looking up, thanks to all the prayers.

I went to my Primary Care doctor for itching and she said it was not yeast infection but was dryness from menopause and suggested I use vaseline for skin and she did a blood test for my estrogen level, which I wanted to know about regarding taking hormone therapy. I also asked her to send Dr. Resta my report from my last Dexa scan and she discovered it was taken over 4 years ago, so she scheduled another one to see if I had osteoporosis. The estrogen level for post-menopausal women can be from 0-31 and mine was 18, which is not very high. The Dexa scan showed no osteoporosis or osteoperina . . . . absolutely normal.

The regular 28 days of radiation was finished on Monday. I was having quite a lot of burning under my arm and the skin was somewhat black. and the scar under my arm purplish. Doctor said I needed to get more air at it, so have been trying to sit with my arm up to give it air and I'm still using aquaphor on it. Last week, the doctor marked the place where the booster treatments would be, around the tumor site and the technicians set up a special arm, measured and made a cut out of the area to be done, then they made a special plate to put in the machine. On Tuesday, they used this for the radiation treatment. This section in the machine was right up close to my breast and I had to turn my head to the side so they could place it, with my special plate in it, where the radiation needed to go. It only took a minute or so of radiation each of the four days. When I finished on the 23rd the area was red all over and kind of white right near the incision and it was sore. Was I happy to be done!

It is now about 10 days later and the black part under my arm is peeling off is about 80% gone and area is just a little sore at times . . . . there are parts still sore to the touch. The incision on the breast part is still somewhat sore but a lot better than it was . . . all seems to be healing. Still having trouble sleeping, have to sleep on the couch as I cannot lay on that breast and still need to keep my arm elevated somewhat.

Our daughter and hubby and grandchildren came for New Years Eve and Day and I had to hold grandchild on right side as it was sore for her to lean against my left side. Plus the weather with snow storms has the fibromyalgia flaring. Was so good to see them, wish I had felt better, but this too shall pass.

Don goes for the laser tomorrow at 6:45 AM . . . praying all will go well and we can get packing to go to Florida . . . The 12th of Jan I go back to radiology doctor for a re check and hopefully start out around the 15th heading south.

We finally left for Florida and while there I was able to start a prayer group in the park before we left in May to come back up north and start with all the doctor visits again. All went well with the eye doctor and the oncologist and the radiation therapist and then I had to return to the cardiologist just to check me out again, as they could not do too much before we left for Florida, because they could not put the leads on my skin for an EKG but gave me an echocardiogram and ok'd me for Florida. Well that appointment went well she did an EKG and all looked ok but she said "let's just do a stress test to check and be sure all is ok." On June 21st I had another mammogram and all was well there. Praise the Lord!

On June 28th, 2006, I had the nuclear stress test . . . My cardiologist was unable to make it for the stress test as she was put on bed rest a few days before as she is pregnant and has to stay on bed rest till she has the baby in August. So, Dr. Mark Nelson filled in . . . I had the test and the doctor had left before the last pictures were done. So they sent me home and Don and I went to lunch and then went home to a message to call the nurse back where I had the test. When I did, she told me that my test results were not good, there was a problem. Could I come there in the morning when the Doctor would be there again to talk to me? We went the next day and he told us I had a very serious problem and that I needed further testing and would need to have a heart catheterization but there was a new non invasive procedure I could do. He sent us to his office in Albany where they took some blood and did the procedure that morning and we met with Dr. Nelson again, the next afternoon and they determined I had a total blockage of the left descending coronary artery along with 2 other coronary arteries being severely diseased . . . and that I needed to have a heart catheterization. It was too late in the day to schedule, as my appointment was late because of an emergency earlier, so by the time we saw the doctor and decided, the staff had gone home in the transfer scheduling area. Went back to office on July 3rd to schedule and I gave more blood. On July 5th they did the Heart caterization which was scheduled for 1:30 PM. I had to be there for 12:30 PM at Albany Medical Center with Dr. Delago who had read the CT scan previously. It was a lot easier than I thought. Afterward, Dr. Delago said that he could not do anything (angioplasty, or stents) as I needed to have either triple or quadruple bypass surgery. That the one coronary artery was 100% blocked and the two other coronary arteries were both 90% blocked. To go home and take it real easy and I would get a call for the next step. Was finished with the heart cath at 2:30 PM and went home at 4:30 PM. Heard nothing that day, Cindy called about 9 AM the next morning and said she just had a feeling they had called. She was on her way to work. We said no not yet but would call her as soon as we heard. After she had hung up, it wasn't 5 minutes when the phone rang and I said to Don, Cindy was right. Sure enough, it was the doctors office and they said I have an appointment with the surgeon Dr. Gerald Sardella on July 12th at 12:15 PM and that after that appointment I would go in the transfer area and they would schedule my surgery and all the tests I needed to have the day before surgery. Meanwhile, I went forward in church and they laid hands on me and prayed.

Received a phone call on Friday, July 7th that the doctor's office had an opening with another surgeon, Dr. Lewis Britton in about an hour from then, so we called our daughter Jodi and she came to the appointment with us. The doctor gave me a physical and then talked to us about what needed to be done and the quality of life I would have if it was not done and I really had no choice. So they scheduled Monday the 10th for the testing at Albany Medical Center. Then to come in early Tuesday for the bypass surgery on the 11th. Praise the Lord, a shorter time to wait and we all liked the surgeon. Soon I will get some sleep while they work on me and then the recovery time. He said that I would probably need only two bypasses but it may be more when he got in there. I was low risk for the operation as my heart muscle was good and except for my other problems I was in good health. He also arranged for all the tests and a leg mapping for harvesting my veins for the bypass.

What a scary time this was, everything was happening so fast but as they said, the sooner the better, before I had a heart attack. I was kind of numb, too much to think about.

On the 11th of July 2006, Jodi and Don brought me into Albany Medical Center real early and they prepared me for surgery. As they were putting a port in my neck, I was awake and the person putting it in was hurting me. There was another doctor there telling him "that is why I don't do it that way" and it dawned on me, the one doing my port was learning and I spoke up and said I did not want anyone practicing on me. I had signed a paper to that effect and was not supposed to have someone learning. They just ignored me, except the man doing it kept saying he was sorry and the other doctor just kept telling him what to do. Again, I said he was not supposed to be practicing on me. I was really upset. Then they put me out. The operation went well but they had to put me on the heart/lung machine during the operation. They put my ribs back with wire and said that the wire would stay in there permanently. They used a mammory vein and also a vein from my left leg. I was in ICU for a little over a day as they did not have a bed for me in the cardiac unit. It was a very difficult time, as I was told I could not use my hands or arms to sit up and I could not lift anything for 6 weeks. I did not realize how much you use your hands and arms to sit up or stand. I think that was the toughest part of the whole recuperation along with not being able to do anything. Thank God for my husband, Don and my daughters Jodi and Cindy. Cindy took time off of work and her husband Chuck, was so good to help take care of their three children by himself at night and his Mom and Dad during the day while he worked, while she came to be with us for a few days after I was released from the hospital. She cooked and cooked and made up several different meals and froze a lot for us to have after she left. Jodi helped do may other things and was a big moral support for Don and I. She also came by and started walking with me to give Don a break.

While in the hospital I had several visitors that really lifted my spirits even though I was heavily medicated.

One day, when I was really down, after I was home about a week or so and still in a lot of pain, I had visitors, Pam & Angie, who are two of my favorite people. They brought food from several at the church and a gift. The greatest gift I received from them was their love and laughing and friendship. They are precious young ladies who are sisters. The joy they brought with them was so encompassing. They started kidding me about my beautiful white stockings I was wearing (elastic to keep clots from forming in the legs.). I had shorts on and the white stockings went up to my knees and they had holes in the bottom and were trying to figure out what they were for. We laughed and laughed some more. It was such a memorable time for me as the "laughter relaxed the brain and short circuited the pain". The Bible says a merry heart is good medicine. They have no idea how much their visit and the kidding and compassion and prayers did for my body, mind and spirit. Sometimes people minister without knowing it and they sure did. Thank you Pam and Angie for being such a wonderful part of my life. I still laugh when I think of their visit. You have no idea and they don't either, what a blessing it was for me and how much it lifted my spirit. Before they left they prayed for me, my husband and family. Another day, Barb stopped by and lifted my spirits with her thoughtfulness and love. How blessed I was for them giving so generously of their kind, joyful and loving spirits. I hope that I can do the same for someone else one day and pass it on.

What God gives to us, is not for us to keep for ourselves, but to share with others or pass it on. Our son in law's sisters husband is an EMT and she is a nurse and they answered any questions I had and came and checked my leg for infection and when I had an irritation in my neck Rick came to check it after work and found they had left a stitch or part of one in my neck where the port was inserted. So he used his medical equipment to take it out and clean it. What a blessing that was to me as it felt so much better and it was the beginning of the weekend. So many special people the Lord has allowed in my life. I am grateful.

After about 4 ½ weeks, they said I could use my hands and arms again. Praise the Lord! Was I happy about that. I was still having problems with my leg leaking where they took the vein. Had it looked at several times. It was kept clean and there was no infection, it just took it's time to heal. Finally after about 8 weeks or so it finally stopped oozing and healed up. I had gotten my walking up to 60 minutes a day and before we left for Florida cut back to 45 minutes a day 4 or 5 times a week. It was suggested that I take physical therapy. When I went to be evaluated I was told I really did not need it as I was doing much more than most of her patients, as most of them do not even try very hard to walk, etc. So I declined taking it as it was for 7 weeks and we wanted to go to Florida in about 3 weeks. However, I did follow everything that was laid out for me by the hospital and the Cardiac doctors.

Praise the Lord, here I am a little over a year later and the cardiologist ordered another nuclear stress test to check my heart. Would you believe it was not good again? I had a part that showed a blockage near one of the grafts so they scheduled a heart catheterization to check it out for September 20, 2007 at Samaritan. Was in by 7 AM and they got me ready. It took two tries to get the port in my arm. It was difficult because they have to take the blood pressure and do everything in that one arm because of the breast cancer surgery on the other side. Finally got it situated and they had someone ahead of me, so Don & I chatted. Then they took me in the OR and got me positioned and then sedated, (the best part). When I awoke after a few minutes they gave me some water and then some fruit and yogurt. I had to wait a few hours for the femoral artery to heal before I got up. When all was done I got up and slowly got dressed, etc. Then the doctor came in and told us I had a blockage and would need a stent. He asked if we wanted to see and we said yes, so he brought us into another room where the pictures he took showed on a screen. We asked how could this happen so quickly after having open heart surgery and he never got a chance to really answer as I felt like I was going to pass out. I guess I should not have been standing so long and they had given me a lot of plavix (blood thinner) which I had never taken before. So they put me in a chair and got a stretcher, put me on it and brought me back to the cubicle I had been in and put me back on the heart monitor, the oxygen and tried to get the port back in my arm. After the second try again, they got it in the elbow and used a wrist blood pressure cuff. The feeling passed and they had me stay another two and a half hours. What they suggested was that on Monday I would have another heart cath and they would put a small stent in and I would stay overnight. It could be one kind of stent that I need to take plavix for 30 days or another kind with medication on it that I would have to take plavix for a year. I had to check with the eye doctor, regarding my macular degeneration, which I did, and he said right now my eyes are not bleeding so there should be no problem. The plavix won't make them bleed it is just if they are bleeding they would bleed more. So I feel better about that. Still have questions but took the doctors recommendation of the medicated stent as he said they were having better results but I would have to take the plavix for a year. Meanwhile, I need to take it easy for a few days until next time.

Been a tough one this time, but, I have the victory in Jesus! Monday, September 24, 2007, I went to Albany Med. At 10:15 AM, was checked in then gave my insurances and paid the balance due after insurances for the overnight stay. All papers were put in a welcome booklet, then I was sent to the cath lab where I was told I would be all set as I just had blood tests last week and an ekg due to having the other heart cath at Samaritan this past Thursday. Sadly, they could not put a stent in as they are not licensed for it yet, which I did not know about until they were ready for the procedure. The doctor had not informed me of this fact. So consequently, two heart caths instead of one but the first one was much better than this one.

Got to the cath lab and they said I needed blood tests and I had to wait for the results to come back before I could have the cath done and stent put in. They also informed me that I needed to have an EKG even though I had one done last week. By the time I got done with all the stuff I was late for my time to go in the OR which was supposed to be 11:30 AM. They finally took me in about 12:45 PM. Same doctor, no problem there, but this time I felt and remember a lot of what they did and especially the closing, the pain was excruciating. Then after they closed the wound it was oozing and they could not stop it right away so they had to put pressure while I was awake and then put some device on me that used air pressure to keep the pressure on the wound while the one nurse was putting pressure and they got that going and she could let go. I asked the anesthetist why she did not put me out and she had some excuse, that some people react differently to medication etc, and the time it takes to take effect . . . (this is a teaching hospital and I think that is what happened) I had just had it done 3 days before and did not feel any pain and woke up back in cath waiting room. After they had that pressure harness on me for awhile my leg muscle started burning and the pain was unreal, so they finally let up the pressure some and that was better. I had to lay like that for two hours or more while waiting for a room. When I finally got the room the packet that I had was with my chart on my lap when the man that transported me to the room gave both to the desk. I asked him about this and he said he gave it to the desk with the chart. So, I thought, well maybe they need it for something.

I will not go into every detail but there was hardly any sleep that night as someone was screaming all night and my roommate snored all night so I maybe got two hours sleep intermittently between all that and taking blood pressure, drawing blood etc. for myself and my roommate each at separate times and only one thing at a time so someone was turning on the lights every half hour or so during the night.

In the morning I was told I could leave at 9:30 AM after the PA came in to see me. She said it would take an hour of paper work and I could leave to go home. Don was there at 9:50 AM and we had to wait and wait and were not able to leave until 12:45 PM. I asked where my booklet was with my papers and receipts and they said they could not find it someone must have thrown it away. We were not happy campers and all I wanted was to get out of there. Just before I left they found out why I was so very sore. It was from the tape, it had ripped my skin right where the groin and inside of the leg meet there were deep ridges about 3 inches long. They called pharmacy and could not get neosporin or anything like it, as the pharmacy did not have it so they put vaseline on a gauze pad so that my underwear did not rub. I started putting neosporin on it myself when I got home it was still very sore. I asked for prayer as I was trying to forgive all the things that happened. I really went through the mill and was totally exhausted. I finally slept some. Am feeling better, it has been a very trying time.

If it were not for the Lord and my family and my church family who supported me in prayers, visits and food for us all, I do not know what I would have done. Through all of this, God has made me stronger both physically and spiritually. He has supplied all my needs. He was there all the time walking right with me and also carrying me through the dark times. I am alive because God revealed the breast cancer before it could go anywhere and because of that they checked out my heart with an irregular EKG but nothing else showed on the echocardiogram and more EKG's but God gave wisdom to the doctor to have me take a nuclear stress test just to rule everything out and be on the safe side. Thank you, Lord, as I would probably not be here today. The greatest miracle of all is, that if I had died, I know I would be with Jesus and I am totally at peace knowing I have been redeemed by the blood of the Lamb. It is by God's grace, love and mercy that I am still alive and it is free to us all. You can have this assurance also, by doing what I have done and acknowledge that you are a sinner and ask Jesus to forgive you of your sin and cleanse you and make you whole. Ask Him to come into your heart and be Lord of your life and teach you His ways and help you to be obedient to His Word in Jesus' Name. Ask Him to fill you to overflowing with the Holy Spirit that your eyes be opened. Then start reading the Bible, God's Word and He will open new doors for you. As you go to Him, He hears and answers in His perfect timing. Keep your eyes on Jesus and you will never go wrong.

I pray as you read these words that you open your heart fully to Jesus and let Him love you into His Family.

P.S. On September 5th, 2008 I had my mammogram and an ultrasound and they found something in the right breast this time so they did an MRI on September 9th. I had an allergic reaction to the dye they injected (which never happens) and had hives, red all over and my face was swollen a bit. Don & I spent an extra hour sitting there after I took some benedryl and they checked me every few minutes and gave me water to drink to flush the stuff out and then I was good to go. Praise the Lord! The results: No sign of cancer in either breast, everything was just fine. Praise the Lord!

72

MINISTER

In the winter of 2006, the Lord spoke to me about becoming an ordained minister. I could not go to college or school for this as I do not drive and due to the Fibromyalgia and other problems where I could not attend regularly. Well, the Lord made it possible for me to take Bible courses at home, which I did, and fulfilled all the requirements. In May of 2007, I was ordained as an independent Christian clergy. I am not quite sure why this was necessary in my life but wanted to follow God's leading. Did not feel I was to be a Pastor of a church, necessarily, but to be able to minister to those in nursing home and other places as He leads me.

I have preached a few sermons in our Church in the Park where we live in Florida from October thru April. With His help and grace I have learned to sing in front of others and even solos.

Before we left for New York in April of 2008 a lady called

(who is also a minister) and said she had seen my name for Bible Study and wanted to know if I would be interested being a part of a ministry to people in an Assisted Living facility located just across the main street from our Mobile Home park. I told her I would get back to her in the fall when we returned.

Meanwhile, I prayed about what to do and the Lord said that is why He has prepared me so when we returned I contacted her again. She asked me if I would go with her while she did a service and we would have communion and she would give short message and asked if I would do a Healing Service afterward. So, we both ministered together and laid hands on each person there as I prayed for their individual healing, body, mind and spirit. What a wonderful blessing it was and I am looking forward to going again this coming month.

Our God is an awesome God and if we just listen and obey, He will not only bless others through you but you will be totally blessed yourself as you reach out to others in His Name and for His Glory!

Here are a few of the sermons I shared . . .

Read Scripture . . . . John 17:1-26 3/18/2007
3 Questions for you . . .

1.   Do you believe Jesus was born of a virgin?
2.   Do you believe He was crucified, died and was buried and rose from the dead?
3.   Do you want to be a child of God . . . a joint heir with Jesus? Romans 10:9, 10-

Prayer is one of my ministries. I believe God has called me to pray for others for healing. There are many types of healing . . . the most important healing is spiritual healing. Having a right relationship with God by repenting of your sin (that means turning away from it) and giving your life over to Jesus. There is also a healing when you have drifted away from God after accepting Jesus into your life and you rededicate your life to Him.

Then there is healing of the mind whether it be from grief, anger, unforgiveness along with so many others. There is also healing of the body from sickness and disease. God can use us to pray for others, especially for healing but He is the only one that can heal if we give ourselves totally over to Him. Sometimes we need one kind of healing more than another and God knows which we need more but He always answers . . . sometimes yes, sometimes no . . . sometimes right away and sometimes it takes a long time but He does answer. God loves you He wants you to be His child . . . He wants those who have drifted away to come back to Him. He does not leave us we leave Him. His arms are open wide to you. Will you come to Him? He does not leave us we turn from Him.

I always thought I knew Jesus but I knew all about Him. I had read about Him, learned about Him . . . Heard about salvation and thought I knew Him until I surrendered my life to Him and He came into my heart . . . then I got to know Him personally. By the power of the Holy Spirit I have read the Bible God's Word and learned to know more and more and love Him more and more.

His arms are open wide . . . the song softly and tenderly Jesus is calling we will sing next . . . Listen to it carefully and decide what you would like to do

AFTER SONG

If you would like to Accept Jesus into your heart or get closer to Him and give Him you all . . . would you and those of you over Channel 96 repeat this prayer after me.

Dear Jesus,

I am sorry for my sin. Please forgive me for anything I might have done, said or even thought that was not pleasing in your sight. Come into my heart and be Lord of my life from this day forward. Cleanse me from all my sin. I surrender all to you. Fill me to overflowing with your Holy Spirit and guide me in my walk with you. I ask this in Jesus' Name. I thank you for my salvation the greatest healing of all.

All those who have sincerely prayed this prayer whether here or at home on channel 96 just raise your hand please. That is putting into action what you have confessed with your mouth. God sees your raised hand and honors it.

Let me pray for you . . . . Lord, I humbly ask that you touch each one who has raised their hand fill them with your love and power. Fill them to overflowing with the Holy Spirit and fire . . . to keep them as your children . . . In Jesus' Name. Amen

Now I Am going to ask for those who want prayer to come forward for healing whether it be for your body, mind or spirit. Come, and allow God to love you. Like the song says rise and be healed in the name of Jesus.

THE DOCTOR KNOW IT DIET 4/15/2007

HEALTH QUESTIONS AND ANSWERS . . .

Q. I've heard that cardiovascular exercise can prolong life; is this true?

A. Your heart is only good for so many beats, and that's it. Don't waste them on exercise. Everything wears out eventually. Speeding up your heart will not make you live longer; that's like saying you can extend the life of your car by driving it faster. Want to live longer? Take a nap.

Q. Should I cut down on meat and eat more fruits and vegetables?

A. You must grasp logistical efficiencies. What does a cow eat? Hay and corn. And what are these? Vegetables. So a steak is nothing more than an efficient mechanism of delivering vegetables to your system. Need grain? Eat chicken. Beef is also a good source of field grass (green leafy vegetable). And a pork chop can give you 100% of your recommended daily allowance of vegetable products.

Q. What are some of the advantages of participating in a regular exercise program?

A. Can't think of a single one, sorry. My philosophy is:

No pain . . . . GOOD!

Q. Is chocolate bad for me?

A. Are you crazy? HELLO . . . Cocoa beans! Another vegetable!

It's the best feel-good food around!

Q. Is getting in shape important for my lifestyle?

A. Hey, "Round" is a shape!

Well, I hope this has cleared up any misconceptions you may have had about food and diets. Now I Will give you one great exercise:

> Begin standing on a comfortable surface, where you have plenty of room at each side. With a 5 lb potato sack in each hand, extend your arms straight out from your sides and hold them there as long as you can. Try to reach a full minute, and then relax. Each day, you'll find that you can hold this position for just a bit longer. After a couple of weeks, move up to 10 lb potato sacks. Then try 50 lb potato sacks and then eventually try to get to where you can lift a 100 lb potato sack in each hand and hold your arms straight for more than a full minute. (I'm at this level) After you feel confident at that level, put a potato in each of the sacks.

Some of those questions and answers are truly funny but as we can see Dr. Knowit doesn't really know it all. He is an example of how, we as people want to be in control. We want what we want, when we want it and do not want to wait or work at being well. We just want to do our own thing at the expense of our health and well being. Sad to say that includes me.

Isn't that what we do in our spiritual lives too? We think we can make it on our own. We want to be in control. We want to take every short cut we can . . . expend the least amount of energy and expect God to be pleased with us. God never said living a Christian life would be easy. But, we can make it! We cannot make it alone. We have to let go . . . give it over to God and with His help we can make it. We can do all things through Christ. I am not saying it is easy . . . believe me I know . . . but by putting our trust and our lives in His hands He will bring us through anything and everything

We began with the heart question . . . . LET'S SEE HOW IT RELATES SPIRITUALLY. Before we can do anything, we need to have our heart right with God. The only way to do that, is through Jesus. It is so easy that it is hard for us to do. This is where your life changes.

That decision is the most important one you will ever make . . . inviting Christ into your life. You can just say, Lord Jesus, I admit I have sinned against You. I am sorry for my sin and I trust You to forgive me. Come into my heart and life and help me to serve You all the days of my life. Amen. It is as easy as that if you really mean it. Not just saying the words, but believing He will.

Then, trust God's forgiveness 1 John 1:9 says "If we confess our sins, He is faithful and just to forgive us our sins and purify us from all unrighteousness." Then declare your faith in Christ . . . Matthew 10:32 says "Whoever acknowledges Me before men, I will also acknowledge him before My Father in heaven." We can then Grow by reading God's Word . . . 1st Peter 2:2 says "Like newborn babies, crave spiritual milk, so that by it you may grow up in your salvation."

Romans 5:1-5 "Therefore, since we have been justified through faith, we have peace with God through whom we have gained access by faith into this grace, in which we now stand. And we rejoice in the hope of the glory of God. Not only so but we also rejoice in our sufferings, because we know that suffering produces perseverance; perseverance, character; and character, hope. And hope does not disappoint us, because God has poured out his love into our hearts by the Holy Spirit whom He has given us."

Gladys Hunt writes:

We now have access to God. Becoming a Christian has enormous consequences. Relationships are changed; we are given privileges; we look at life different; our resources are inexhaustible. How do we receive all of this? Paul makes this clear: through our Lord, Jesus Christ. (Romans 5:1)

Our relationships are changed: we have peace *with* God (Romans 5:1). When we are at odds with God, inner peace eludes us. Becoming a Christian necessitates being made right with God, and what a difference it makes! *Peace with God* is enough to sing about!

We are given privileges: we have access by faith into God's very presence (Romans 5:2). Once we knew only hostility; now we are invited into the King's presence. Once we were outside; now we are welcome inside. Access. What are you doing, with the privilege, of coming into God's presence?

We look at life differently: we can be joyful even when facing the hard things that come into our lives (Romans 5:3). We know life isn't purposeless. God is taking the stuff of our lives and making something good out of it. We are on our way somewhere. God wants to get us ready for heaven. Our joy is real, because we know, we will one day, share the glory of God.

Our resources are inexhaustible: God keeps pouring His love into our hearts (Romans 5:5). He not only makes us feel very loved, but He is so generous in His supply that we have an overflow of love for other people. He gives us the Holy Spirit, who not only transforms our thinking, but makes God's love real to us.

Our trouble begins when we forget these great realities and concentrate on our inadequacies, our fears, and all the other manifestations of our smallness. The proof of God's love is that Jesus Christ died for us. We are no longer shivering outside in the cold, with no credentials, to come before the King. Jesus, has invited us, into His very presence, and has given us, all we need, and more besides. This passage in Romans 5 is a renewed invitation to take advantage of your privileges as a daughter or son of the King!

Another answer given by Dr. Knowit, was . . . . No pain . . . .
Good!

I am sure many of you would love to say that! I would too! And I am grateful for days that are less painful in my body or mind than others. I am also very thankful that the Lord gets me through one day at a time. Beginning in summer of 2003 Don was diagnosed with prostate cancer and had a seed implant and radiation treatments. Summer 2004 I was diagnosed with Macular degeneration had laser surgery then when the eye started bleeding again we had to go back up north. Summer 2005 Don had cateract surgery on both eyes about a month apart and is being treated for glaucoma. We were ready to go to Florida and I had my Mammogram just before we were to leave and they discovered the breast cancer. Summer 2006 we discovered I needed Open heart surgery. We have been through a lot together but not at the same time, thank God. We took turns. If it wasn't for God's help and the prayers of God's people . . . I do not know where we would be.

One thing I do know that no matter what was happening . . . by being obedient to God's Word and following James 5:13-16 which says "Is any one of you in trouble? He should pray. Is any one happy? Let him sing songs of praise. Is any one of you sick? He should call the elders of the church to pray over him with oil in the Name of the Lord. And the prayer offered in faith will make the sick person well; the Lord will raise him up. If he has sinned he will be forgiven. Therefore confess your sins to each other and pray for each other so that you may be healed. The prayer of a righteous man is powerful and effective."

I know this is true as I had macular degeneration the wet kind that bleeds in the eye. They wanted to operate on the eye right away when my eye started bleeding again but I said no and we went back to New York to see the doctor there. I lost the central sight in one eye but was prayed for before I went to the doctor and I did not need laser treatment to stop the bleeding or an operation as it had stopped before I got there. I was also diagnosed with macular degeneration in the other eye but now they are both very clear and that was the Lord's touch. Then when they told us I definitely had breast cancer I went to the elders of the church the Sunday before the lumpectomy and they prayed. During the operation they found no cancer in the surrounding tissue or in the lymph nodes. Praise the Lord! After about 3 weeks or so I started my 42 treatments of radiation which was scary but with God's help got through it. When they had this big machine over me and the noise it made and being in the room by myself, I was really afraid I would keep saying Jesus . . . Jesus . . . Jesus and He got me through . . . . I am totally clear of cancer! While putting me through tests before the Lumpectomy they noticed something different on my EKG. I had to go to my regular doctor to check it out before they would admit me. The doctor ok'd me for surgery but told me I had to go to a cardiologist before we left for Florida. She could not do an EKG as I was still having radiation but they did an echocardiogram and said it looked ok but after we get back to come see her again. When we got back from Florida in spring of 06 . . . . They did an EKG and echocardiogram and everything looked ok again but decided to do a stress test just to be on the safe side. After the stress test Don & I went out to lunch. When we got home our answering machine was blinking. I checked the messages and the nurse had called saying to call as soon as we got this message. When I called she said "I hate to tell you this, but when we checked the films we saw that you have some severely blocked arteries and you need to come back and see the doctor right away as this is very serious. He has left for the day but will see you first thing in the morning. What a shock that was! Needless to say we did not sleep much that night. We went back in the morning and the doctor told us that I had blockages in my heart and he gave me several medications to take and told me I could not do anything or go anywhere as I could have heart attack at any moment . . . . Scary . . . . you bet! That Sunday they laid hands on me and prayed. More testing showed 100% blockage in one large artery and two others 90% blocked. They tried heart catherization. They were unable to fix it that way so I had to have open heart surgery. But I only had to have a double bypass as one of the arteries had grown its own new arteries to supply blood to that area of the heart. Praise the Lord! Scary . . . . but with God's help and many prayers, here I am. Praise the Lord! He is faithful . . . . we just have to trust Him.

I have said many times why me? I do not understand why these things happened. In 1st Peter 1:3-9. It says "Praise be to God and Father of our Lord Jesus Christ! In His great mercy He has given us new birth into a living hope through the resurrection of Jesus Christ from the dead and into an inheritance that can never perish, spoil or fade . . . kept in heaven for you, who through faith are shielded by God's power until the coming of the salvation that is ready to be revealed in the last time. In this you greatly rejoice, though now for a little while, you may have had to suffer grief . . . in all kinds of trials. These have come so that your faith . . . of greater worth than gold, which perishes even though refined by fire . . . may be proved genuine and may result in praise, glory and honor when Jesus Christ is revealed. Though you have not seen Him you love Him; and even though you do not see him now, you believe in Him and are filled with an inexpressible and glorious joy, for you are receiving the goal of your faith, the salvation of your soul.

I do believe God cares about every little thing that happens to us and He will use it for good. Romans 8:28 says the following . . . "And we know that in All things God works for the good of those who love Him, who have been called according to His purpose." I cannot tell you how many people have come into my life who also have Fibromyalgia. Because I have dealt with it since 1987, I can understand how they feel and what they are going through. The various people I have met and shared with during the whole process of finding out I had cancer, through the operation and radiation treatments. Then those regarding my heart operation and recovery to share with others in the same situations. What a privilege to be able to encourage and pray for someone and say yes, I have been there, I understand your fear or frustration and what you are going through. I have been able to share with them and now with you that no matter what the circumstance, no matter how you feel, God is right there by your side . . . through it all . . . waiting for you to ask for His help. His Word is true. He did it for me . . . He'll do it for you. He is no respecter of persons. God loves you just as much as He loves me. We are precious in His sight. He loves you! He wants only good for you. You can make it, With God's help . . . Will you let Him?

CATCHING UP

A lot has happened in my life since 2010 when I first published this book. A heart cath with a stent in 2012, cancer in the right breast with a lumpectomy followed by radiation in 2016. Another heart cath with stent in 2017. Cancer in left breast for second time with lumpectomy and radiation treatments following in January 2021. Slight heart attack October 2021 with two heart caths no stents. Cancer again for 3rd time in left breast, 4th overall, lumpectomy on October 25th, 2022. No additional treatment.

They were calling me Joblina, due to my past and all that was happening during the last year or two. During this time my husband Don's prostate cancer returned as they found it in his sacrum (the bone in the lower back and in his lymph nodes. I was his sole caregiver at this time. It was a very hard time for him and for me. He was dealing with the cancer having treatments with chemo pills and hormone injections as well as side effects which were embarrassing for him and he could not go out and enjoy himself as he had no control over anything. It got to the point he could not drive which was very difficult for him as I have not been able to drive due to my many health problems. Although I can drive my golf cart in the Park.

During this period I have also been Associate Pastor to our Church in the Park as well as being Secretary, etc. Our Pastor had fallen and broken his femur and was in rehab for quite a while for that and for his heart conditions.

Also, my oldest daughter found out she had breast cancer and had a double mastectomy with reconstruction. She needed to have chemo for several weeks and then graduated to shots every three weeks and hormone therapy pills. All three children came to visit their dad and she came in between her treatments. Then we found out the youngest daughter had breast cancer also so she had a double mastectomy with reconstruction and was waiting for a surgery date so she came down to visit her dad with her sister and Don was not doing good and was on Hospice. While they were here Don fell and I had to call 911 and they brought him to the hospital to check him out. They found out what was causing one leg to swell the hospice nurse thought it was the lymph nodes but they found a blood clot was causing it and they said it would really be bad if it was in the lungs so they wanted to check that before they released him and they found out it was in the lungs. They released him to a hospice care facility as I could not take care of him anymore.. The girls were both here and my son had been here a few weeks previous. The girls stayed with him at night at the facility. They both had to finally go home as both had to deal with their cancers. Two days later my husband of 56 years went home to be with the Lord.

Was this a hard time in my life - Yes it was.. BUT - I have the Lord, I had people praying for us all and HE brought us through every circumstance. There were days I called out to Him and said, "Lord, I can't do this anymore!" HE would say to me, "Yes, you can." "Only with You, Lord" I would say and the next thing I knew I had the strength to go on. My slight heart attack was during this stressful time of caring for my husband and that gave me a break for a few days of rest with my children coming and helping. They were here when Don fell and went to the hospital and then to the hospice facility. It has been hard on all of us but God has given us grace and mercy and joy in Him. I am totally at peace. He has been with me every step of the way. Prayer and giving it to the Lord is the key. HE lifts the burden...one day at a time.

The surgery I just went through, I continue to be totally amazed at how great I feel. A little sore but in less pain than I had before surgery. I had such peace. They wanted to do a total mastectomy so I prayed but I did not have a peace about it. When I decided to do the lumpectomy or partial mastectomy instead I had such a great peace I just knew I was doing the right thing for me at this time. God is awesome! He did not say we would not have troubles and trials in this world but He did promise if we look to Him, He would get us through and that He would never leave us nor forsake us. I am rejoicing! Four times I have had breast cancer and each time it was caught early on Mammograms. Get yours!!! I praise God for that and now I am cancer free in Jesus' name! Hallelujah!

I am thankful for all the prayers of friends and family and those who have reached out in love. Thank you, Lord, for your goodness and mercy. What He has done for me, He can do for you. Once you have reached out to Jesus for forgiveness and invite Him to be your Lord and Savior, He hears and answers, for it says in the Bible, "Ask believing and you shall receive." I am so blessed as I have received many times over and He keeps giving and giving in so many ways.

God does answer prayers. He does care about every little thing and big thing that happens to us. HIS love is never ending!!!

In August of 2023 Pastor Bill retired and the congregation voted that I be the new Pastor for our Church In The Park. It seems like the Lord has been preparing me for this for years. I am so blessed by the Lord and the people in this church. I am so happy that I can serve the Lord in this or any capacity. To God Be The Glory!!!

I could not do it without HIM!

THROUGH PROSE . . .

Serena Johnson's

Poems

VALENTINE PRAYER TO JESUS

When to my heart, I asked you in
I was mired deep in sin.
Your life you gave that I might live
So, Lord to you, my life I give.

I love you, Lord, with all my heart
With all my soul and mind.
Please, dear Lord, I beg of you
Don't let me fall behind.

Open my ears to hear your voice
And ever be secure.
Open my eyes as I read your
Word And help me to mature.

Praise your Wonderful, Holy Name
For all you've brought me through.
I'll sure rejoice when you say . . . .
"COME"!
And I'm face to face with You!!

FAITH

Jesus was crucified
Bless His great faith
Jesus died on the cross
To our great dismay
Jesus rose from the dead
Praise the Lord, we say
Do you have faith in the Lord?
Do you have trust in the Lord?
Do you praise and thank the
Lord each and every day?
Do you try to live
As the Lord wants you to?
Jesus did so much for you
For Him, what will you do?
Are you willing to walk His way?

PATHWAY TO GOD

Love is the key, for you and me,
Keep the faith, stay in His grace.
Try to help in ways that you can
Show more love for your fellow man.
Keep the Path to God free!

Pray to God, every day
He will help guide the way.
Read the Bible for His Holy Word
Then remember what you have learned.
Turn to Christ and repent!

Give Him your love, with a free heart
His love for you will never stop.
Spread His goodness throughout the world.
Inform the people of all His works.
Show your love to God!

QUESTIONS

Did you smell the roses today?
Did you hear the wind?
Did you feel the warmth of the sun on your face?
As another miraculous day begins.

Does the dew glisten as the light from the sun,
Reflects rainbows of color from the heaven's above?
Contemplate the beauty and wonder you see,
Listen . . . . as the birds sing their sweet melodies.

Alone in the garden Jesus waits for you and for me.
Will we take the time to sit at His knee?
Will we let Him love us and set our hearts free?
His compassion is boundless, on this we agree.

Come as you are—no need to pretend,
Just sit and talk to your Wonderful Friend.
No matter the problem . . . He understands,
Give Him your love . . . put your life in His hands!

A GENEROUS SPIRIT

So often it is easier to be generous than to accept generosity from others. But the ability to let someone else find joy in our pleasure—is what really takes a generous spirit. For in letting others help us, we are giving up a little of our pride and allowing our human vulnerability to show through. This is true generosity—giving another person the opportunity to touch our lives.

JESUS SAYS:

"You can be sure that on the Judgement Day everyone will have to give account of *every useless word he has ever spoken*. Your words will be used to *judge you*—to declare you either innocent or guilty." Matt. 12:36, 37

"If you *forgive others* the wrongs *they have done to you*, your *Father in heaven will also forgive you. But*, if you *do not forgive others*, then your *Father will not forgive* the wrongs *you* have done." Matt. 6: 14, 15

JESUS SONG

Jesus, all I want is Jesus
Always there beside me
Lighting the way

Spirit, blessed Holy Spirit
Sent to guide me day by day

(refrain) Jesus, oh, oh, oh, oh, oh, Jesus . . . .
How you bled and died for me
To take away my sin 2x

Jesus, how I love you Jesus
Lord, you mean so much to me
More than I can say

Father, how I love you, Father
You sent your son Jesus
That we may live

Jesus, let your love flow through me
To reach out to others
So they may be saved

Father, Son, and Holy Spirit
Thank you for forgiving
Touching me with love

Teardrops, flowing like a river
Cleansing and forgiving
Mistakes that I've made

LET JESUS IN

To tune: Let the sunshine in
Many times we're troubled
Or, we may have sinned,
Put your faith in Jesus
And you will always win.
We should think of others,
Help when'er we can,
Should not be so selfish,
Try to understand.

REFRAIN:
So, let His love flow in,
Always think of Him,
Open up your heart and le et Je sus in.

Open your heart and mind' Keep all your goals clear.
Try to be real cheerful, To whom ever's near. He is
always watching, Waiting with His love. In deeds we
can all show Him, Our hearts have opened up.

I'LL KNOW I'M HOME

The Lord is there Just and fair
His love you see
Jesus died for thee
To set us all free

CHORUS:
By your love I'll know I'm home
Then my heart will never roam.

Forgive all my wrongs
I'll praise you in song
I'm at your command I know you understand
Thanks for holding my hand.

In my heart come
Jesus, God's only Son
Never leave, please stay
I'll do it your way
Born again, you say.

There's love at last
Forget the past
You've set me free How can I thank Thee
Peace, Love and Joy You give me.

Love one another You say
For everything pray
I'm a child of the King
That's the song I sing
When my room's prepared, He'll ring . . . .

ANGELS
by Serena M. Johnson

There are angels all around you,
Even though you cannot see.
God has given them assignments,
To protect both you and me.

As we seek our paths on earth,
We may wander to and fro.
The angels are beside us,
No matter where we go.

Thank you, Lord, for your protection,
As I go along life's way.
May my life be pleasing in your sight,
Each day, I humbly pray.

AT THE BEACH
by Serena M. Johnson

Cars are parked all in a line,
The sun is out, the clouds divine.
Sand dunes standing straight and tall,
Sea oats waving, one and all

Along the walkway peek flowers bright,
Purple and blues, what a wonderful sight.
See the waves and bear them roar,
Then lap peacefully at the shore.

See the beauty of land and sea,
That God created for you and me.
Miraculous creations within my reach,
Whenever I wander along the beach.

Beauty, How Precious

by Serena M. Johnson

Blue the skies, foamy green seas,
The beauty of the earth I see.

Colorful flowers pop up as I pass,
Vivid green fields, ripple with grass.

After thunderstorms clash, with driving rain,
An awesome rainbow in the sky again.

The wind is whistling through the leaves,
Warm sunshine on my face, does please.

Moonlight shining down at night,
All the stars are twinkling bright.

All this beauty, you gave, for us to see,
Thank you, Lord, for your love so free!

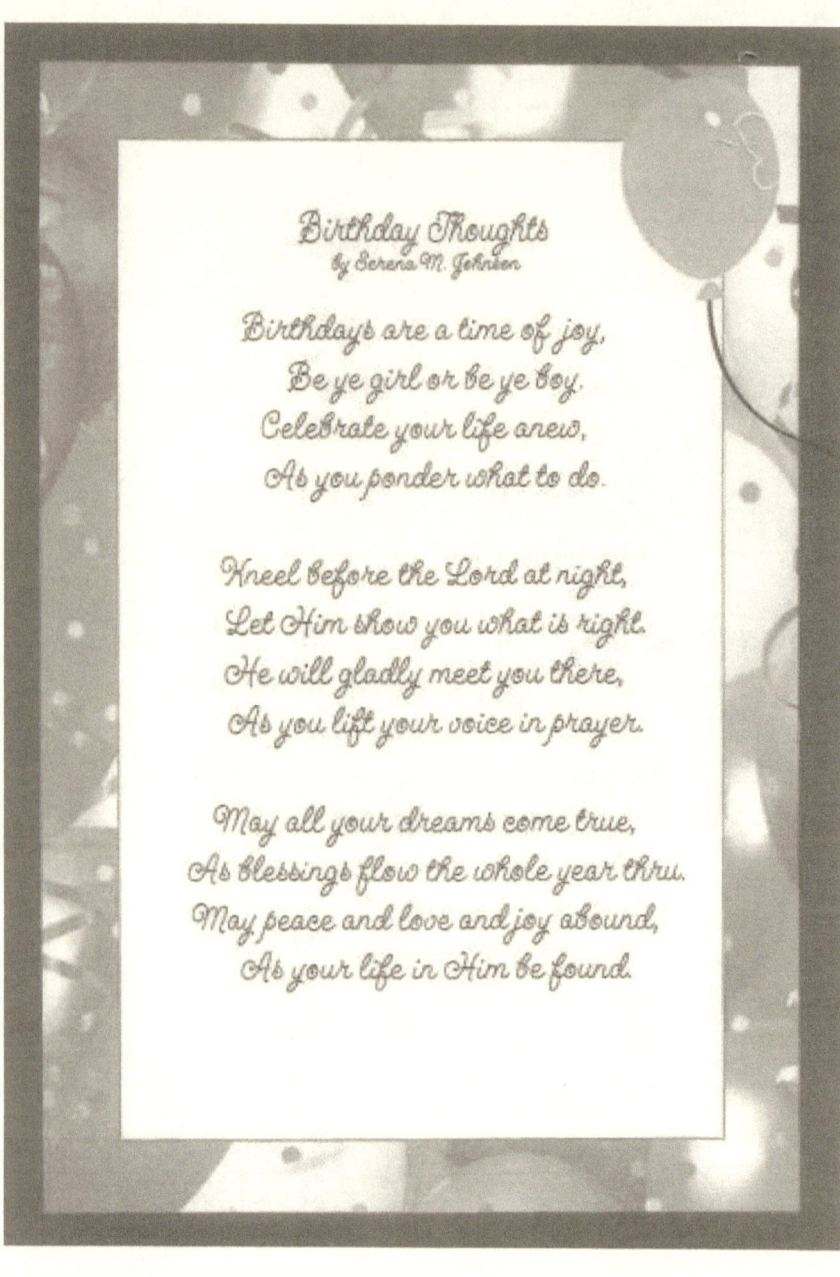

Birthday Thoughts
by Serena M. Johnsen

Birthdays are a time of joy,
Be ye girl or be ye boy.
Celebrate your life anew,
As you ponder what to do.

Kneel before the Lord at night,
Let Him show you what is right.
He will gladly meet you there,
As you lift your voice in prayer.

May all your dreams come true,
As blessings flow the whole year thru.
May peace and love and joy abound,
As your life in Him be found.

CALLED
by Serena Johnson

You bid me, walk on water,
You calm the angry sea.
You call us sons and daughters,
Your love has set us free.

You say we are forgiven,
If we turn to Thee.
The life that we are living,
From evil we shall flee.

My heart is Yours, my Jesus,
How can I ever thank You?
For I am Yours forever,
You bless me in all that I do.

Refrain:
You have called,
I have chosen,
To be Your child,
My heart is open!

CHANGING SEASONS

by Serena M. Johnson

The sun reflects the colors gay,
As the breeze rustles the leaves by day
When the grey dusk comes, it brings the cold,
After brief touches of frost the leaves grow old.

As time creeps along, and our winter begins,
The leaves, plucked from their branches, by the wind.
This beauty is gone, when the north winds blow,
But then comes a many patterned blanket of shimmering snow.

The naked trees have donned new coats of white,
Can't you just picture this wondrous sight? At
night you walk as huge flakes increase,
So clean and white, it gives you a feeling of peace.

CHRISTMAS

by Serena M. Johnson

The sun peeked through on this blissful morn,
The day when Jesus the Christ was born.
The cattle in the stable lowed,
The donkey brayed, and was there snow?

Mary looked upon her wondrous Son,
His life on earth has just begun.
Joseph stood and faced his bride,
His smile was beaming, bright and wide.

How could they know what was to come,
The life and death of their dear Son.
Forever grateful we shall be,
For Jesus' love for you and me.

CHRISTMAS JOY
by Serena M. Johnson

There He lay upon the hay,
The Magi sought Him day by day.
The wondrous child, it was foretold,
Would come to earth and save our souls.

Jesus lived through many storms,
The Son of God in human form.
Remember that His Word is true,
And He is reaching out for you.

Forgive me, Lord, for all I've done,
Come in my heart, and it's begun.
My life I freely give to Thee,
Thank you, Lord, You 've set me free.

CREATION
by Serena M. Johnson

Beneath the canopy there is a breeze,
As sunlight filters through the trees.
The colorful birds in trees above,
Singing sweetly, their songs of love.

Can you hear the symphonic sound,
As the rushing water swirls around.
An eagle soars, a lion roars,
As pelting drops of rain doth pour.

As a rainbow bursts forth across the sky,
We know, upon His promises, we can rely.
How lovely is Your creation's view,
Lord, all our praise belongs to You!

CROSSING OVER

by Serena M. Johnson

Many years have come and gone,
My heart is weak, my bones not strong.
All the pain just lingers on,
Take me home where I belong.

Refrain: Crossing over peacefully,
To the land beyond the sea.
For His blessed face to see,
I hear Jesus calling me.

See my body lying there,
Surrounded by all those who care.
Jesus, all their sorrows bear,
Let them not be in despair.

Oh, the light of love and grace,
As I'm taken to that place.
Joy and peace that I can taste,
As I behold Your blessed face.
After last refrain:
Hallelujah! The blind can see!
Hallelujah! The deaf can hear!
Hallelujah! The lame can walk!
Hallelujah! MY JESUS IS HERE!

DELIGHT IN THE LORD

by Serena. M. Johnson

My child behold the time is now
Time to reap and time to plow.
Time to hold you in Mine arms
So, my child, don't be alarmed.

My love for you forever grows,
as I listen to your prayers.
When you worship at My feet,
Mine eyes are wet with tears.
Be vigilant, My child,
to always come to Me.
In trouble, joy or pondering
and sit upon My knee.

I long to have you visit
and ask that you would stay.
Seek Me first, in all things,
I will show the way.
My help, My love, My wisdom,
to you I will impart.
Giving, always giving,
from deep within My heart.

GIVING ALL

by Serena M. Johnson

Alone or afraid, whisper His Name,
Jesus is there, always the same.
He is with you from the start,
Gives you peace within your heart.

Jesus, Redeemer, Savior, Lord,
Let us be in one accord.
Following You, I will be blessed,
As You give my spirit rest.

Take away my doubt and fear,
Help me wipe away my tears.
For I know Your Word is True,
So, freely, I give my life to You.

God's Son
by Serena M. Johnson

You formed Him in the womb.
You raised Him from the tomb.
When they came to the Inn,
They said they had no room.

The manger was His bed.
That's where He laid His head.
Herod wanted to kill this child,
But God raised Him up instead.

Jesus came to set us free.
They hanged Him on that tree.
He bled and died upon that cross,
To save both you and me.

What the Bible said is true.
He did it for me and you.
To make our path to Father God,
and our relationship renewed.

Jesus

HEART ACHES

by Serena M. Johnson

Your love was nailed upon that tree.
As You bled and died for all to see.
You paid the price, you set me free,
So that Your love could flow through me.
My life to you I freely give,
Show me, Lord how I should live.
Thank you, Lord for all you do.
My heart is free when I praise You.

Weave Your love into my heart,
So we shall never be apart.
Allow Your peace to flow through me,
Let Your light shine for all to see.
My heart rejoices when we meet.
Lay my burdens at Your feet.
Stand beside me, hear my plea,
Help me, Lord to be more like Thee.

Thank you, Lord, for all you do,
Help me, Lord, to follow You.
My heart rejoices when I pray,
As you stand beside me day by day.
My life to You, I freely give,
Show me, Lord, how I should live.
Clear the path and help me be,
All that I can be for Thee.

HEART TO HEART
by Serena M. Johnson

I look at you and now I see,
A child whose fall of love for Me.
From morning light till end of day,
You think of Me, and often pray.

My heart is full of love for you,
It pleases Me, you love me too.
Be bold my child, and come to Me,
For only I, can set you free.

He's There All The Time
by *Serena M. Johnson*

Into our lives some rain must fall,
And just when you think you have it all,
The wind comes crashing in the squall,
But Jesus is there, our All in All.

When dark clouds turn to gray,
Or when you are caught in the fray,
What must we do without delay?
Bow our head, it's time to pray.

Take my hand, as I reach out to Thee,
Take my heart, it's yours, and set me free,
Allow Your love to blanket over me,
As You live in me for all to see.

His Hand
by Serena M. Johnson

There is a mighty wind that blows,
Sparkling gems ride the ocean waves that flow.
There are sun kissed, lovely skies of blue,
With puffy clouds that float there too.
There is rain that patters through the gloom,
As flowers raise their heads in bloom.

Oh Lord, I see your mighty hand,
Has touched this earth and it is grand.
We see You in all things below,
May Your light and love through us show.
You made this world so I might see,
The love and peace You have for me.

I AM WITH THEE

You will know that I am with thee
You will see Me in the clouds
I shall be your Consolation
Every minute, every hour.

Keep your eyes upon Me, Jesus
And I will show you how
To practice what I'm preaching
So that I can use you now.

Every knee shall bow every tongue confess that I am Lord
I am with you even though there will be discord
Follow Me, As I will lead you
Thus saith the Lord

I am with thee, I am with thee
Many gifts and promises don't deny
On My Word, you can rely

I am with thee, I am with thee
All the sins of My people
Only make Me cry.

As My tears do turn to gladness
. . . . This can be
For if you tell them of salvation
I will draw them unto Me.

In His Arms
by Serena M. Johnson

I wonder, I wonder, as I go along.
I see all the beauty, in every song.
I'm singing Your praises, from dusk until dawn.
In the arms of my Savior, is where I belong.

Oh, just hold me tight, Lord, please don't let me fall.
I love you, Lord, and I will answer Your call.
Because of Your mercy, now I can stand tall.
Know that now and for ever, You're my All in All.

Allow me, Lord Jesus, to love you today.
Be ever beside me, as You guide my way.
Oh, cleanse me and heal me, and use me I pray.
For enclosed in Your arms, is where I want to stay.

Refrain:
Come hold me, enfold me, for I am Your child.
Let me bask in Your love, as I rest in Your arms.

I THANK THEE, JESUS

Dying for me to be saved . . . .
and the Comforter you gave, I thank thee
Coming back from above . . . .
and your overwhelming love, I thank thee
The times you were denied, the tears that you cried,
I thank thee
My sins you took instead . . . .
the blood that you have shed, I thank thee
The forgiveness that is mine . . . .
your glory divine,
I thank thee
You died for me upon that tree,
I thank thee
So blue the sky . . . the birds that fly,
I thank thee
For all the beauty you allow me to see
I thank thee
In mansions tall . . . . there's room for all,
I thank thee
You show you care . . . . You answer prayer
I thank thee
The gifts you give . . . . That I might live,
I thank thee
The life you gave . . . that I be saved
I thank thee

THE MIXTURE OF MARRIAGE

You start with a large dose of love,
Add in as you go along.
Have faith and trust in Him above,
You'll never be far wrong.

Always add some encouragement to your mate,
Although at times it may be hard to do.
In disagreements or stress, to talk it out will make,
The situation brighter, as understanding comes anew.

With this mixture in your marriage . . . now and always,
Which we know you two will find.
Blending your individualities, through the days,
Will enrich you and together, you'll have a life sublime!

MORE OF YOU

by Serena M. Johnson

With your healing arms around me,
Your strength, gets me through the day.
As I feel Your love surround me,
You are with me, as I pray.

Let my life be one of giving,
All to you and less of me.
Help me be a willing servant,
Thankful You have set me free.

Give me wisdom, love and mercy,
As I live my life in You.
Lead me, Jesus, by Your Spirit,
In everything, I say and do.

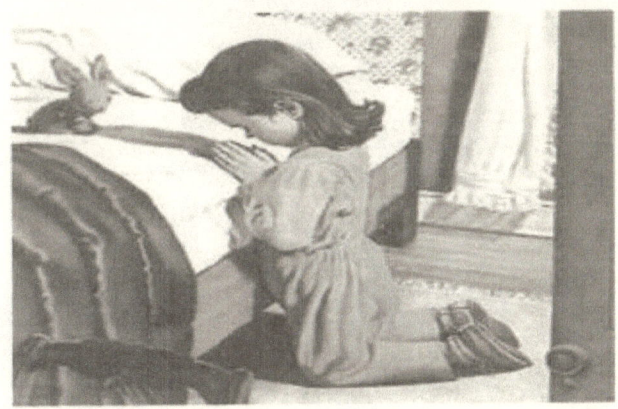

MUSINGS

by Serena M. Johnson

As I cross over,
I walk on water,
then I step upon the clouds,
I am guided by the sunbeams,
As I reach,
the throne of God.

As I leave, the world
behind Me,
All the pain, and
grief are gone.
I hear the music,
and the singing,
with the angels all around.
HIS wondrous love, envelops me,
as to HIM, I humbly bow.

MY ABODE
by Serena M. Johnson

As you step inside:
May you find His peace.

As you sit awhile:
May you be covered in His love.

As you leave this place:
May the fullness of
His joy abound.

As you walk in His grace:
May His blessings freely flow
to you and through you

MY FURRY FRIENDS

by Serena M. Johnson

I have some kitties, as cute as can be,
Who like to jump and climb all over me.
When I call, they make me wait,
But, time for treats, they're never late.

They scoot up here, and zoom over there,
I hold my breath and pray they land with care.
I hear a crash and laugh to see,
They scared themselves, as well as me.

Even though at times, I's like to give them away,
But, oh the joy I feel, as I watch them play.
They jump in bed, snuggle close and purr,
Always wrapped around my heart,
as I stroke their real soft fur.

MY PROMISE

Raindrops fall upon us all,
Do not stumble, lest you fall.
My heart is sad, for those who sin,
For My Spirit is not within.

Lend your ear and hear My plea,
I have come to set you free.
Do not worry, or be afraid,
If My Word you will obey.

Come, My child, and sit with Me,
Allow your burdens all to flee.
Put yourself into My hand,
I shall come and heal your land.

smj

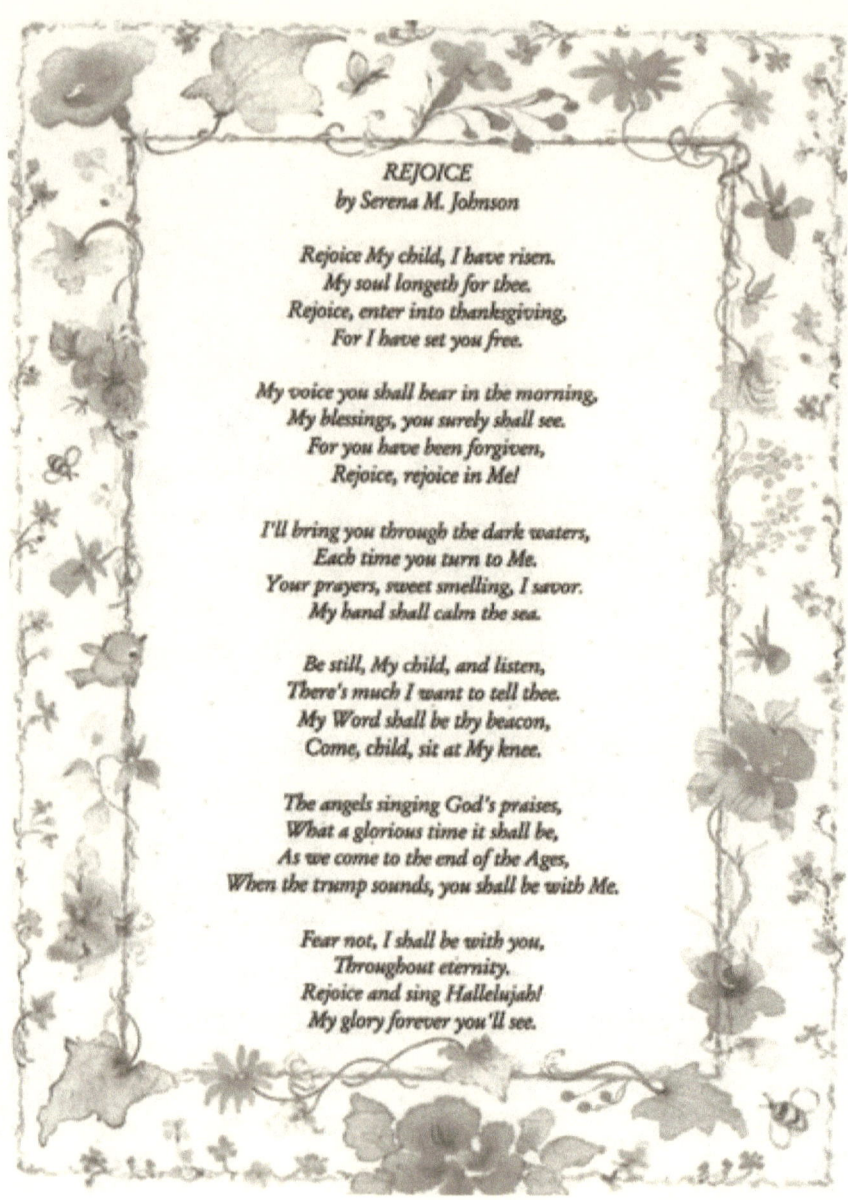

REJOICE
by Serena M. Johnson

Rejoice My child, I have risen.
My soul longeth for thee.
Rejoice, enter into thanksgiving,
For I have set you free.

My voice you shall hear in the morning,
My blessings, you surely shall see.
For you have been forgiven,
Rejoice, rejoice in Me!

I'll bring you through the dark waters,
Each time you turn to Me.
Your prayers, sweet smelling, I savor.
My hand shall calm the sea.

Be still, My child, and listen,
There's much I want to tell thee.
My Word shall be thy beacon,
Come, child, sit at My knee.

The angels singing God's praises,
What a glorious time it shall be,
As we come to the end of the Ages,
When the trump sounds, you shall be with Me.

Fear not, I shall be with you,
Throughout eternity.
Rejoice and sing Hallelujah!
My glory forever you'll see.

REVELATION

These are hard and troubled years,
Striving for independence and seeing Mother's tears.
Seeking desperately to find your way,
Experimenting and living day by day.

One thought that will usually arise,
Why don't parents agree with what I decide?
They complain and put my way of life down,
What I'm doing is done the whole world round.

They are trying to tell me what I should do,
It sometimes seems like I'll never get through.
There is one thing deep down I could not bear
SILENCE—Oh, God, that's the reason, THEY CARE!

SING PRAISES

by Serena M. Johnson

The birds sing sweetly in the trees,
As Jesus says, Come follow Me.
Listen, do you hear the song,
As by the tree you walk along.

My body hurts, my pain increased,
Lord, will you give me Your great peace?
I put my life into your hands,
Allow my mind to understand.

Let me sing a song to Thee,
Like the birds up in the tree.
Allow my praise to you be free,
Will You live inside of me?

THE FLOW OF LIFE

by Serena M. Johnson

In the meadow there is a little brook,
That sighs as it merrily rolls by.
As I sit and dip my feet and look up,
I see puffy white clouds and clear blue sky.

I wonder as I'm sitting there,
What is God doing in Heaven so high.
Is He watching over me,
Listening to my cry?

Oh, Lord, I feel unworthy,
But through Jesus, you've shown me how.
Let my lips sing praise to you,
Allow my prayers, to please you now.

As this flowing brook, dear Lord,
My faith and hope renew.
Here is my heart, my mind, my soul,
I give it all to You!

THE LIGHT IS THERE

God's light doth shine
On this humble heart of mine
My pathways are not always bright
But with His help I've seen the light.

Reach inward, search the depths of your mind
Then outward to God whose love you'll find
No matter the nature of what you defend
Upon His presence you can always depend.

Seek Him out not only in times of trial
In the midst of joy and peace you can smile
Remembering that God is at work in His own ways
Deserving eternally our daily praise

Thank you, Lord, to my delight,
I'm able to see your shining light
Help others to search their heart, open themselves to giving
And let in Your light and love for a wondrous new beginning.

WAVES

by Serena M. Johnson

It slowly rises, gathering...
Power, as the wave takes wing.
Then you see the frothy foam,
As it crests and rolls alone.

Thundering waves break at the shore,
As we wait and watch for more.
The sky so blue, you hear the sound,
As white fluffy clouds surround.

See the palm trees gently sway,
Beckoning forth a glorious day.
Lord, Your creation, so beautiful to see,
As the warmth of Your love encompasses me.

WERE YOU THERE

(words for Christmas)
by Serena M. Johnson

Were you there when Jesus Christ was born?
Were you there when Jesus Christ was born?
Oh, Oh, Oh, sometimes it causes me to ponder, ponder, ponder.
Were you there when Jesus Christ was born?

Were you there when the star would lead the way?
Were you there when the star would lead the way?
Oh, Oh, Oh, I feel the wonder, wonder, wonder.
Were you there when the star would lead the way?

Were you there when they came the Wise Men three?
Were you there when they came th4e Wise Men three?
Oh, Oh, Oh, it causes me to fall upon my knees.
Were you there when they came the Wise Men three?

Were you there to see the Savior's face?
Were you there to see the Savior's face?
Oh, Oh, Oh, it causes me to hunger, hunger, hunger.
Were you there to know you are saved by grace?

What's New?
by Serena M. Johnson

What have we gone through, day by day,
Have we tripped along the way?
Made some headway can we say,
Upon HIS shoulders our burdens lay?

As the old year comes to an end,
What will the new year bring, my friend?
Are peace, love and joy around the bend?
HIS love for you will never end.

Do not wait another day,
Come to Jesus without delay.
All your fears HE will allay,
Give to HIM your heart today.

ARTICLES OF INSPIRATION AND REVELATION

YOU'LL NEVER WALK ALONE
(words for Christmas)
by Serena M. Johnson

When you feel you cannot go just one more day,
Ask th4e Lord to come into your soul..
Jesus will help you, He'll show you the way,
He'll be with you wherever you go.

the Refrain:
Walk on, walk on, with God in your heart
and you'll never walk alone.

EXERCISING FAITH

Sermon: 10/28/2007—Serena Johnson
Hebrews 11:1 "Faith is the substance of things hoped for
the evidence if things not seen." Matthew 14:22-31
These were all disciples the Lord asked to get into the boat. First
Peter asked Jesus if he could come to Him Jesus said Come!
When Peter got out of the boat he had put faith into action
by trusting Jesus at His Word. When he looked at the
surroundings and thought about it logically, he sank.
Even with Peter's lack of faith for a few moments, Jesus
still had compassion on him and lifted him up out of
the water. He did not leave him or forsake him.

Faith asks in prayer and seeks God's will.
Then waits on the Lord
And trusts Him and obeys His Word.

Christ is always the goal. To be like Him.

Many Christians are waiting for God to move in their life, to
make some dramatic change, to open doors to greater power or
ministry but yet spend all their time doing worldly things.

They are so busy doing other things they do not spend time
with the Lord. They participate in gossip, they let anger,
unforgiveness and bitterness or jealousy and what about ME
rule their lives instead of being obedient to God's Word.

I am as guilty as the next person . . . . How I was upset with the people in the hospital and how I had to forgive them.

Here are a few examples of what God says about this:

Luke 6:27-36 (Love for enemies)

Matthew 18:15-21 (Brother sins against you)

Matthew 6:9-15 (Lord's prayer)

BEFORE we pray we need to be cleansed from all unrighteousness.
Then we can ask and expect to receive. That is
what God's Word says . . . . not me.
The first thing you need to do is ask Jesus to be your Lord and
Savior . . . that is the greatest healing of all. That
allows us to get in the boat (the Family of God)

Healing Thoughts and Prayers Scripturally

Are you ready to step out of the boat and be healed? Jesus is
saying "Come, His arms are open wide for us. We need to put
Jesus FIRST! Ask Him if we should get out of the boat. We need
to believe His Word and Trust Him and if we hear Him say
Come,

GET OUT OF THE BOAT!

If He is speaking to you now and you believe He wants to heal
you in your body, mind or spirit, let's pray and ask Him to
forgive you for the things you have done or said that was not
pleasing in His sight. Ask Him to heal your unforgiveness, anger,
bitterness . . . we cannot do this alone, we need His help.
We'll pause for a moment while you Reach
out to Him! Lay it all at His feet.
Now, Put action to your belief that He does
want to touch you and make you whole.
Will you come for prayer?
He is here ready to meet your need. Let Him enfold you in His
arms.
He loves you, He wants to heal you. COME!

ARE YOU FORGIVEN, CAN YOU FORGIVE?

Sermon 4/11/2010

With this being Appreciation Sunday, as much as I appreciate all of you, there is one, whom I appreciate, most of all. His Name is Jesus. The Easter passion reminds us of what the Son of God did for us by taking our sin upon Himself and suffering and dying on the cross and then rose from the dead so we could be reconciled to God the Father. Until I came to the realization that He did that for me, personally, and really understood that even if I was the only person created, He did it for me . . . . Serena Johnson. It is an awesome reality to know that He loved me that much. Through Him I was set free from sin and death. Because I asked Jesus to come into my heart and be my Savior and Lord and forgive me for all my sin, I have been forgiven. Have you?

Throughout my life since then . . . there have been many temptations, trials and tribulations and He has gotten me through every single one. Why? How? Because He touched me! (Sing song: "He Touched Me")

When I accepted Jesus as my Lord and Savior in 1979, I was struggling with many things from my past. Don and I had been married for 14 years at the time and we were raising three children and I was working part time and Don was working many long hours.

During this time I had met this woman who sold Avon door to door (short testimony . . . see page 44) As you can see I desperately wanted to be close to the Lord and be His child.

Some of the hardest things the Lord has shown me I needed to do was to forgive my x husband, forgive God that my baby died, and forgive myself. I thought my baby dying was my fault . . . that I had done something wrong so I was being punished and I held a lot of guilt.

During my first marriage I carried my first child, Daniel for 9 months and he died at 2 ½ days old of a cerebral hemorrhage.

My x husband was an alcoholic and abusive. One night when our second child, Shawn, was 5 months old my x came home drunk. Shawn was crying as my x was yelling etc. and he went over and yanked our son by his hands out of the crib. Talk about an angry mama bear . . . after I told him not to move, I gently took Shawn out of his hands and comforted him and put him back in his crib. Then I went and pounded my x on the chest and told him to get out . . . that he could hurt me all he wanted but he was not going to hurt my baby! He left and did not come home that night and I called my parents and in the morning had help to move Shawn and myself out to live with my parents. Found out he was seeing another woman and I filed for a divorce. So much hurt and anger . . . so much I had to work through.

In 1964 I met Don and in December 1965 we were married. Don has been and still is one of the biggest blessings God has put into my life along with our family. I am very thankful for Don, as we have been through so much together in the 44 years we have been married. By the grace of God and His love, we made it through each and every obstacle along the way.

The Lord's prayer reads:

> Our Father who art in heaven hallowed be thy name, thy kingdom come, thy will be done on earth as it is in heaven . . . give us this day our daily bread and forgive us our sins as we forgive those who sin against us and lead us not into temptation but deliver us from evil for thine is the kingdom and the power and the glory forever . . . amen.

If Jesus forgives us like we forgive others . . . where does that leave us? Are you forgiven? Can you forgive?

ONLY through Jesus' love can we be forgiven or are we able to forgive others . . . How do I know? Because many times I have had to forgive others as well as to be forgiven. I was able to forgive because I made the choice to ask Jesus to help me. What a burden I had carried and what freedom I was given when I let go and let God.

The Word is true . . . Come to Me, all you who are weary and heavy laden and I shall give you rest. Lean not to your own understanding, in all thy ways acknowledge Me and I shall direct your path

God wants us to live in love and have great peace and joy and the only way you can have that is to trust Him to lead you and guide you and help you each and every day to live as He would have you live. Not forgiving will eat at you and make you sick and then it spreads to others around you.

Take this scripture with you as you dedicate your life to the Lord Jesus and let Him love you and show you a way to peace. Jesus said the greatest commandment in Mark 12:30 "The Lord our God is one Lord . . . Love the Lord your God with all your heart and with all your soul and with all your mind and with all your strength. The second is this: Love your neighbor as yourself . . . There is no commandment greater than these."

Forgiveness is not about forgetting . . . It's about letting go of another person's throat . . .

Whoever you are angry with is God's child . . . His creation, He loves them too and wants to redeem them.

Forgiveness does not establish relationship . . . In Jesus, God has forgiven all people for their sins against Him but, only some people, choose a relationship. Forgiveness is an incredible power . . . a power we share with God, a power Jesus gives to all He indwells, so that reconciliation can grow. When Jesus forgave those who nailed Him to the cross, they were no longer in His debt or God's. God will never bring up what they did or shame them or embarrass them.

Forgiveness is first for you, the forgiver . . . to release you from something that will eat you alive, that will destroy your joy and your ability to love fully and openly.

God wants us to take on the nature that finds more power in love and forgiveness than in hate.

When you forgive . . . you release that person from judgement, but without true changes no real relationship can be established. It doesn't require us to pretend it never happened . . . but you can love in the face of it.

Forgiveness does not require that you trust the one you forgave. But, should they finally confess and repent, you will discover a miracle in your own heart that allows you to reach out and begin to build between you a bridge of reconciliation.

At times this may seem impossible to you . . . but nothing is impossible with God. The road may even take you to the miracle of fully restored trust.

Your burden can be lifted by going to God and asking His forgiveness first. We have that choice. He will help us forgive others if we just lay this at His feet and choose to forgive as Jesus did for us.

"Do unto others as you would have them do unto you" . . . the golden rule is something we can live by. To live as free people in Christ and love one another as Jesus loves us.

In Mark 11:25 Jesus says: "And when you stand praying, if you hold anything against anyone, forgive him, so that your Father in heaven may forgive you your sins."

Think about it! It is very important that we forgive, so we can be forgiven. This verse has really hit home to me . . . has it you?

Unless we accept forgiveness from Jesus, we cannot truly forgive others and if we do not forgive others once we have accepted forgiveness from Jesus then our sin after we accepted the Lord . . . will not be forgiven.

We block our own paths by holding onto resentment, anger and unforgiveness. Just like when we eat junk foods that cause buildup in our arteries and make us walking time bombs on the verge of a stroke or heart attack leading to death. Unforgiveness can lead to spiritual death, for it can block our love and peace when we are not trusting God and following in His Word and His Way.

Do you have unforgiveness in your heart for someone or something? Your husband, wife, child, your job, your church, your doctor, lawyer, your minister or priest, a neighbor or friend? It is not only hurting you, but those around you. Why not cast off the heavy burden and let the Lord help you to forgive and therefore free yourself to live a more powerful, positive and productive life.

Let Go and Let God . . . His Ways are always better!

Let us pray:

> Lord, forgive me for sinning, I am truly sorry. I want to be your child. I thank you for dying on the cross for me and for rising from the dead so that I may be saved and have eternal life. Jesus, come into my heart and be my Lord and Savior. Reveal to me the Truth of your Word and help me to forgive others as you have forgiven me. Thank you, Jesus! Amen.

If you have said this prayer Jesus knows you are sincere and will give you all that you need to forgive others and be forgiven. May you be filled to overflowing with His love, His peace and His joy unspeakable as His blessings rest upon you in Jesus' name and for His glory!

GIFTS

During the time of Christmas, we think of gifts. I'd just like to discuss gifts from God. God has many gifts for us! The first and most important gift is Jesus Christ, whom He gave to us, so that His Son could take our sins, take our sicknesses and diseases upon Himself and bring them to the cross. To shed His blood, to suffer unmercifully at the hands of men and to be willing to die on that cross for us, for our sins, for your sins. If there were just you in this world he would have died just for your sins. That is the greatest gift of all! He died so that you may be saved! Isn't that a great gift?

It says in God's Word, the greatest gift you can give or the greatest thing you can do for a friend is to give your life. That is what Jesus did. He gave His life for you that you may be saved. After this tremendous gift of Jesus dying on the cross, He came back! He was raised from the dead! He went to be with the Father and He came back and told His disciples . . . "Wait and I will send you My Comforter, I will send you the Holy Spirit". He was true to His Word, He sent His Holy Spirit at Pentecost. He sent His Holy Spirit so that His disciples would have the power to go forth and proclaim His Word. Oh, He has so many gifts for us! See: I Corinthians Chapters 12 and 13.

All these gifts, many people say, this one's not important, that one's not important, that's not for today, I don't need that. People believe that salvation is for today but they don't believe that the gifts of the Holy Spirit are for today. Why should those gifts be any different? If none of the things in the New Testament were for today what would be the sense of the Bible at all? God said in His Word that He wishes us to have these gifts. If God did not want us to have these gifts He would not offer them to us. But we say some are less important.

Personally, I feel if God has a gift for me, it is not going to be a bad gift, it's going to be something for me that is good. He only gives good gifts to His children. Something that will make me a stronger Christian . . . . will make me more as Christ would have me be. All the gifts He has to give are for our benefit or others benefit. Who am I, to deny a gift that God's given me, or that He has for me. I do not always know the benefit of the gift, but I want it, because I know through His Word that He wants me to have it.

You have to want what God has for you. It's just like before Christmas, you ask your child to write down a list of things that are most important to them, that they would like to have the most. Why do we do this? Because children sometimes want something they see, and sometimes 2 or 3 days later, they don't really want it or they misuse it. It's not really the desire of their heart. So we wait and give them the chance to search out and find what they most desire. After they've done this, then these children come to you. Mommy or Daddy, "This is what I want. Oh, it would be so great if I could have this!" This is how God wants us to come to Him, as little children saying, "Yes, God I really want this! I really desire all the gifts that you have for me!" Not half-heartedly, not just "If you want to give it to me, I'll take it." He wants to know that we really want all that He has and then it is ours. How Great God is! He has so much to give us if we but open ourselves to Him.

He's reaching out to you to give you these things. Do you turn your back on Him? He doesn't turn His back on you. We don't deserve a thing . . . . we do not deserve a thing! What have we ever done to earn anything that God has given us? Every single one of us is a sinner, saved by grace, by the grace of God we're saved! Praise God! He loves us so much He gave us His Son, He gave us His Holy Spirit, He gave us all these gifts to use for His honor and His glory! Are you using them? Are you stepping out in faith and seeking all that Christ has to give or are you just taking what's comfortable? Are you just sitting back and saying I'm saved . . . Thank you, Jesus, but that's all I want! Or, are you committing yourself, your total self, to God? Are you opening yourself? Oh, I know it is painful at times. It is very difficult when you're confronted with the truth, the truth of knowing that some of the things you're doing are not God's will. And yes, it's so easy to make excuses and say "Oh, I can do that . . . I'm doing it just a little bit . . . . It's not really wrong, I don't do it all the time like other people . . . I try to be good but I'm just human . . . I don't know how to do it . . . I can't show love . . . Let someone else do it." Is that what God wants? No, my friend, that's not what God wants! He wants us to go to Him. He wants us to ask Him for the strength we need and He'll give it to us! If we do not have the love for our enemies, (we don't), through Christ Jesus we can have this love. We have to ask for it! We have to really want what God has for us in order for us to fulfill our promise, our commitment to God.

When you committed your life to Christ, did you just commit and say "What's easy"? Ok, Lord, I want to do what you want me to do . . . but when it gets a little hard or you have to suffer a little bit or people laugh at you or persecute you, do you say "Oh, no, Lord I don't want to do that!" Jesus said "Pick up your cross and follow me." He didn't say it would all be easy. But look what He's given us! For this short period of time even if we have to suffer for His sake we will have eternity to be with Him to share in His riches in glory. Oh, how glorious that will be—for the fulfillment of His gift of eternal life. All the other gifts that He has are to help us. To help strengthen us through Him. To help us bring others into His Kingdom for His honor and

His glory. For we can do nothing without Him but there is nothing that is impossible with Him! "For we can do all things through Christ Jesus who strengthens us." He will guide us, He will give us these gifts if we but turn to Him and earnestly desire to serve Him. I ask you to contemplate these things and most important is Read God's Word! If you have committed your life to Christ then read His Word! If you have said Lord, I want to do what you want me to do, I want to lead the life that you would have me lead. Then read His Word! How else can you fulfill your commitment to Christ. If you do not know what He wants you to do, how can you do it? You must read His Word so that you will know the truth, His truth, so that you know if someone is leading you astray. You must read His Word and then follow. It will not happen overnight, it will take time, but as you walk and as you learn, you will grow. You will grow as a child of the King and you will know that our greatest gift is His Love. And if you ask Him, He will give you the gift of His Agape' Love.

STEWARDSHIP

A few weeks ago I read an article in the paper that one church was accepting pledges through credit cards. This is quite a different way of doing things . . . but yet the concept is good. That is, setting aside each pay day, a certain sum, along with your monthly bills. Your contribution to help further Christ's work through our church. Although our giving of monies is very important, there is something that is more important . . . Giving of ourselves through our time and talents.

When we first came here we were very impressed by this church due to the friendliness and concern of the people toward us (as strangers) and toward each other. This I feel is a great Christian attitude and no matter how big this church may grow I hope we never lose this valuable quality.

As some of you may know I have always been interested in writing and I happened to show some of my stories and poems to one of the members. She told me there was a need for an editor of their newsletter and would I think about giving it a try. Well. I thought about it and it was like God was bugging me so I volunteered to try it. I wasn't sure I could do it but it was worth trying. Well, needless to say, with God's help, I must have done something right because I was editor for several years. The rewards have been many! I got to know more about the church and the marvelous people in it. I never would have made it without the help and support of so many of you.

There was also something else I had always wanted to do and that was to teach children in Sunday School. I was asked but I felt with my Catholic background I wasn't qualified but, through the re-assurance from Pastor and others I made up my mind *to try*; which I did, and it was marvelous working with the children and learning and growing with them.

Through many experiences during the past of being involved and trying new ventures, working for Christ, I have found a great closeness to Him. It has brought a great change in my life, which is hard to explain, but I am more at peace with myself . . . more self-confident. I have more willingness than ever to do what I can to help people become involved and find their way to Christ as I did. So if there is anyone who has thought about doing something to get involved in the church, I urge you to think about my experience and volunteer to try. You may not hit the ideal job that you are suited for the first time but don't ever get discouraged and stop trying. God will guide us to our most effective role in the life of the church. Decide to give of your time and talents, explore new horizons, for it's a marvelous feeling and experience working for Christ.

ONWARD CHRISTIANS

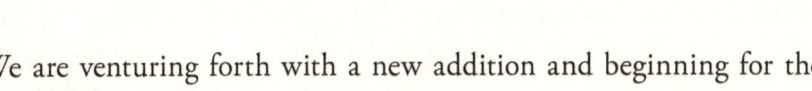

We are venturing forth with a new addition and beginning for the outside structure of our church. It has occurred to me that this is a great opportunity for us to open the door and reach out to others as Christians!

Our past is behind us. Let us remember the good things that have been done and how far we have traveled together. With all of us there may be persons we have had contact with in church, at home, at work, or school, of whom we have formed an adverse opinion. Let us not forget we all have faults and differences, together with our own high's and low's. We can open our minds and hearts and wipe the slate clean and start over. We can try to understand the other person's point of view and give them another chance. We can reach out to new people to make them welcome as well as those already attending. As a Christian, we have the ability to forgive and accept, through Jesus. To denounce, hold a grudge or judge others is so easy to do but it is not what Jesus would have us do. There is only ONE judge.

Can we all honestly say we are being a Christian in our attitudes? If not, then we should examine our consciences and motives and re-direct our energies, through our most precious Lord, that we may all work together in harmony as He would want us to. As each brick is laid it works with the other to lend support to the building. From the smallest nail to the largest beam each one, in itself, is equally important but each depends on the other to give support and strength and so it should be with us as Christians.

We have a new chance, let's take hold of it and stay on the right track and join with one another for our future together as truly united Christians working for and through Christ!

Dear Heavenly Father,

We praise you for who you are . . . and we thank you for your Word and your promises . . . You said, "Ask, and ye shall receive, seek and ye shall find . . . knock and the door shall be opened unto us." Lord, touch each person reading this with the healing they need . . . whether it be in their physical body, or in their mind . . . or in their spirit. In Jesus' Name I ask . . . fervently believing they shall receive. I praise and thank you for the answers, whatever they may be, for I know "All things work to the GOOD of them that LOVE THE LORD and ARE CALLED according to HIS PURPOSES". Amen and AMEN!

TO GOD BE THE GLORY . . . . FOR THE THINGS HE HATH DONE!!

DEBT HAS BEEN PAID

What would you do if after the holidays all your bills that arrive in January had "PAID IN FULL" marked across them? Would you try to find out who paid them and why? Would you tell others about this person? Would you thank God for this person? Would you speak good of this person? Would you thank this person?

Well, that is what JESUS did for YOU! God sent His Son, Jesus, who willingly took YOUR SIN and MINE upon Himself and died on a cross. He died in YOUR PLACE so that you might be saved and spend eternal life with Him. He did this for YOU because HE LOVES YOU . . . . and He loves you JUST THE WAY YOU ARE! If you think you've done too much wrong and sinned so many times that He won't forgive you . . . YOU'RE WRONG. If you feel you have to try to be a better person and clean up your act first or go to a certain church or go to church so many times a year . . . YOU DON'T! For God's Word says "Whosoever will may come". He is calling YOU. If you have drifted away from Him . . . He is calling YOU . . . . NOW . . . TODAY.

What do you have to do? Tell Jesus you are sorry for your sins and ask Him to forgive you . . . . If there are specific things you know you've done that was not pleasing to God, tell Him you are sorry for them and ask His forgiveness. Then invite Him into your heart to be LORD OF YOUR LIFE. Then what! FIND OUT MORE about Jesus. One way to do that is to read the BIBLE (HIS WORD) every day if you can and by the power of His Holy Spirit, He will teach you. Talk to Him each day, He longs to speak to you. He created us that we have fellowship with Him. Be His friend . . . Why not start today?

Has your debt been paid? It's all up to you. He will not force Himself or His gifts on you. You have to want to allow Him to mark your debts (sins) PAID IN FULL and receive eternal life. Ask, believing, and you shall receive. You shall receive the most important gift of your life. As one songwriter put it: "He paid a debt He did not owe. We owe a debt we cannot pay. We needed someone . . . to wash our sins away . . . And now we sing a brand new song . . . Amazing Grace . . . Christ Jesus paid a debt that I could never pay."

May Jesus, the Christ, Son of the Living God, touch each of you in body, mind and spirit, with healing and wholeness and may His love and peace permeate your entire being and bring you rest and joy unspeakable.

NEW BEGINNING

Has this past year been trying? Have you been searching for something to make life worthwhile? Are you sick of this world, your job, your family, your friends? Have they disappointed you or let you down? How would you like a new beginning? Wiping the slate clean, starting all over, forgetting what the past has been.

Get married! What, you say . . . I'm too young . . . I am married . . . . I have no boyfriend or girlfriend . . . You must be crazy! Bear with me.

When you are "courting" or going out with someone and contemplating living with them for the rest of your life you start by an engagement, which says, you will not go out with anyone else . . . . that he or she is all you want. Then you see each other more often, learn more about each other and discuss what you expect from each other in your relationship and your dreams and goals for the future. How you will take care of and love one another plus much, much, more.

Then the day comes that you are both totally in love and want to commit yourselves to each other for life. You have come to the decision that you want everyone to know it and witness it. So you plan to "get married" (commitment). You walk down that aisle and commit yourselves publicly to one another. A beginning of a new life . . . together.

Thus, is the same for you this year . . . . No matter what age . . . What marital status . . . . What sex . . . What you've done in the past . . . What you are doing now . . . . The Bridegroom, (Jesus Christ) is waiting for you to come down the aisle and publicly proclaim, after learning about Him, that He loves you so much He died for you and that after three days He rose from the dead and is alive . . . . waiting for you to come to Him in marriage (commitment). Ask Him to forgive you for the past and tell Him that you want to turn away from your sin and follow Him. That you will put Him first. That He is more important than anything or anyone in your life. "Come to Me all that are heavy laden, and I shall give thee rest"—Walk down that aisle . . . Take His hand . . . Make your commitment to Him publicly and you will experience a new beginning . . . Making Jesus, Lord and Savior of your life. Those who might have been divorced or separated from Him . . . . He's there with open arms to welcome you back for He said "I shall never leave thee nor forsake thee." You can walk down that aisle again and re-marry (re-commit) yourself to Him. Then I guarantee your life will be exciting and adventuresome.

The answer is . . . . Falling in love with Jesus. Not just knowing Him or having a casual relationship . . . just knowing about Him, or just well enough to shake hands with . . . . but literally caring enough to commit everything to Him. Your life will take on new meaning . . . You will be filled with such joy and peace.

Jesus is waiting for you at the end of the aisle . . . Why not meet Him there?

"LOVE ONE ANOTHER AS I HAVE LOVED YOU!"

(Do you have heart failure?)

This verse of scripture is the new commandment Jesus left with us. This Valentine's Day message is for husbands, wives, boyfriends, girlfriends, Mom's, Dad's, each teenager, youth, child, brother, sister, aunt, uncle, grandma or grandpa, young or old. It's LOVE . . . .

People term love in many different ways, Some feel it's giving material things to others. To some, it's to say I love you and holding hands and kissing a lot. Some feel, it's having sex. Others believe it's doing something for someone else. Some don't really know what love is.

"Love is patient and kind; it is not jealous or conceited or proud; love is not ill-mannered or selfish or irritable; love does not keep a record of wrongs; love is not happy with evil, but is happy with the truth. Love never gives up; and it's faith, hope and patience never fail. Love is eternal." (1Corinthians 13:4-8)

How did Jesus love you? He came to earth, born of a virgin. He lived a perfect life and became the perfect sacrifice once and for all, for your sin. In your place, He took beatings, was spat upon, made fun of and then He had nails driven into His hands and feet upon a cross of wood, which afterward was put into a place in the ground for Him to hang there, where He suffered and then died. After three days He rose from the dead and is now LIVING . . . . sitting at the right hand of God the Father. He did all this so that you could be put in right relationship with God. That now, through Jesus, we could come to the Father and we could have eternal life. HOW? By believing Jesus did this for YOU. That He does love YOU that much! He will accept you just the way you are, if you go to Him, and ask Him to forgive you of your sin and ask Him to come into your heart and be Lord and

Savior of your life . . . .

What greater love could one have for a friend but to lay down His life for him. Jesus didn't say . . . . only if you never made a mistake will I love you . . . . He loves you just the way you are!

We all need love and encouragement, support and understanding. If you don't feel you are capable of loving as Jesus loves . . . . YOU AREN'T! But . . . . once you've accepted Jesus into your heart—He will create in you a new spiritual heart and when you ask Him for His agape love to flow through you to others, and believe He will give it to you . . . . He does. Then you too, can be the encouragement, the love needed, the help, the support, the understanding of others, through Jesus' love.

Won't you be Jesus' Valentine . . . . Be a channel of His love. Invite Him into your heart today. "O, God, create in me a new heart and renew a right spirit within me."

You are in Spiritual Heart Failure without Christ. When you allow Jesus to be Lord of your life you receive a Spiritual Heart Transplant!

WHY ME?

What is the reason for my being? I have pondered this question many times throughout my life. Through many heartaches and hurts there has bloomed in my life a deepening love of God. Yes, there have been many times I've turned my back on Him, blamed Him for hurting me and those I love, but He has never forsaken me. He's always been there to give me renewed strength when I've been down. Why should He help me? He needn't as I am not worthy. I am but a mere mortal with may imperfections. Lord, only you, have the marvelous understanding and unending willingness to forgive my failings.

I have found that no one need be alone—ever—for the Lord is ever present in our lives. All we need do is reach out to Him for guidance, strength, understanding and His overwhelming love. It is a great comfort and joy to know in your heart and mind He is always with you. Money cannot buy this, material items cannot attain this . . . . but, faith and trust in the Lord can bring peace and joy beyond measure. I know that I am important to Him and He loves me.

I love you too, Lord, and even though I don't always understand your reasons sometimes, for things that happen, I try to be worthy of your love. Thank you for giving meaning to my humble life.

INSPIRATION

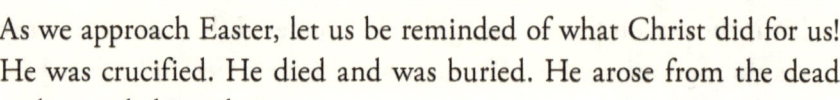

As we approach Easter, let us be reminded of what Christ did for us! He was crucified. He died and was buried. He arose from the dead and ascended into heaven.

Let us all take a good look at our lives. Are you satisfied with the way in which you are living? Do you think the Lord is pleased with the things you say and do? Renew your life! Turn to God for strength and help to live in His image. Seek God's guidance for what you can do through Him to make the world as He would want. If everyone did their part, we all could have a better world in which to live. Find inner peace by doing for others and sacrificing some of your time and talents for Him. Let us be inspired by the meaning of Easter and not just think but ACT!

SEEDS FROM WITHIN

Each of us has many seeds inside ourselves, we have initially the seeds of life, to be able to reproduce ourselves. Then others spring forth as our life begins. We hopefully learn about the seeds of love, to be able to give and receive; concern and caring about others; understanding, being objective when someone acts the way they do or says what he thinks; patience, to take time to sort out what may happen; faith, in your fellow man, in yourself and in God; hope, trying to be optimistic at all times and forgiveness, not to hold a grudge if a situation can truly be rectified by your ability to forgive.

There are always weeds in a garden, thus is so in ourselves. We have weeds of anger that we may feel towards others by constantly finding fault or criticizing. We are unable to accept any sort of criticism ourselves no matter how well intended and we allow anger to come forth instead. Another is selfishness, thinking only of ourselves and not of how others may feel which can eventually grow into loneliness, as there is a limit to patience and understanding in us all. Fear can be a weed, for it can engulf us if we are not able to explore what we fear and confront it, as we may end up with mental and physical anguish and stress should it take hold. The weed of perfection can bring mistrust of people and things and can make us feel nothing will be done right if we're not there and everything has to be done our way. This can also bring us to ridicule and put down others because to us they are different in their looks or opinions.

There are many varieties of seeds and weeds too numerous to mention. The sad part is that weeds can choke off all the seeds if they aren't tended to and a garden of weeds is not worth much and may be passed by. A single seed in full bloom however, is like a ray of sunlight breaking through the dark clouds giving you a glimpse of the beginning signs of beautiful things to come.

Many of the seeds my lay dormant waiting for us to help give them a new start so that they may grow and flourish within us. Can we analyze ourselves as to which we are helping to grow, the seeds or weeds? Are we cultivating the ones we should? It is a constant effort but do we all make the effort or are we sometimes slack and do the weeds overrun the garden? Tact, love and understanding sprinkled daily could provide some nourishment. We also have the unique ability to reach out and be a ray of sunshine in someone else's garden, help control the weeds and stimulate possible dormant seeds so they will bloom again and again.

Only you can decide which will dominate in your life and within yourself. Will it be the seeds or the weeds?

WHAT IS HEALING?

Perfect healing is what God has granted us through His Son, Jesus Christ, who suffered many afflictions, who took every sickness and disease in this world upon Himself. And then, by His own will, was led to the cross, to die on that cross, willingly, for each and every person for their sins, for their sicknesses. He took it all upon Him so that you would be rid of sickness and disease and eternal damnation. Through Jesus, God's Son, His life, and His ministry, and His willingness to go to that cross and take your place, so that you may have eternal life. So that when you die, you will be with Him, be a child of His and live with Him for eternity. This is the perfect healing that Christ has promised us. There are many types of healing, physical, mental and spiritual. In God's Word it says "Seek ye first the Kingdom of God and all these things shall be added unto you." Well the first step to any healing whether it be physical or spiritual is to come to the foot of the cross, to Jesus, to make yourself right with Him, to become a child of the King! How do you do that? Well, before I became a child of the King, I thought I knew God. I thought I knew Him very well and that I was close to Him. I was involved in the church, I was on all kinds of committees and programs, I taught Sunday School . . . did all kinds of works! I would "do unto others as I would have others do unto me", at least I tried. With all this, I really thought I was close to God. Until, I discovered, I really didn't know God at all. I really didn't know that He had sent His Son, Jesus Christ, to die for my sins. MY sins! Why would He die for my sins? That happened a long time ago. Yes, I know He died on the cross and yes, I was taught He was raised from the dead, I believed that! But, I really didn't think about it much. I didn't really know that you could have a personal relationship with Jesus Christ. I finally found out that by my going to Jesus and asking Him to forgive my sins (and we're all sinners). It says in God's Word, "We all have sinned and come short of the glory of God." There was only one man who had no sin and that was Jesus Christ. He was a perfect vessel and He took all of our sins upon Himself. Yours and mine. He did that for us! I had never really stopped and thought about it but when a dear friend told me about this, that He loved me that much, I felt, I'm not worthy. But Jesus didn't say "you're not worthy". He loved me right where I was and when I went to Him and said "Jesus, forgive me for my sins, I am truly sorry. Thank you for dying on the cross for me. Would you be Lord of my life? Would you guide me to do the things that you would have me do?" He was true to His Word. He did come into my life and I praise God that He allowed me to be His child! The joy that comes from knowing Jesus Christ personally, is indescribable! That is the most important healing I will ever have or that you could ever have. If you would like to give your life to Christ and receive this healing, pray the following prayer and believe in your heart: Dear Jesus, I know that You died on the cross for my sins. Lord, I thank You for that and I ask You to forgive my sins. I am truly sorry for anything that I have done that was not Your will. Please come into my life and heart and be Lord of my life. Show me how You would have me live! Lord, I know You were raised from the dead and I know that now I will be with You in heaven for I have committed my life to You. I praise You and thank you in Jesus' name. Amen.

How great it is to serve a LIVING GOD! One who died and rose again. That's a great healing! There are other healings. There are spiritual healings. There are things we must give over to the Lord and ask Him to help us with. Many things in our past have to be healed. Things that happened when we were children. Maybe you were unwanted as a child, before you were even born and this has been a mark on your life. Give it to Jesus. Maybe as you were growing up you were teased or rejected in some way, either at home or at school. Give it to Jesus. Maybe a teacher that criticized or was mean to you. Forgive . . . Give it to Jesus. Maybe there was a time in your life where you were molested. You can have that healing, give it to Jesus. Was there a broken marriage or times when cutting things were said by your husband or wife, mother, father, sister or brother? Give it to Jesus, He can heal it! You have a loved one you had an argument with and you probably don't even remember what it really was about. Jesus wants to heal that relationship. Give it to Him. We must forgive one another, but we, by ourselves, cannot do it but with Jesus giving us the ability, we can. Ask Him, give your problem to Him, get rid of your burdens! Maybe you think your life is not worthwhile, that you cannot do anything right, you're a failure, you are no longer useful, or needed. Not true! Give your life to Jesus . . . He will lead you. He will show you that YOU HAVE a purpose. He loves you. He loves YOU!!! Let Him heal you. You may have physical infirmities . . . Give them to Jesus. Put your life in His hands and when you receive your healing, praise and thank God. Tell others what He has done for you! Give God the honor and the glory, for it is only through Him that we have anything! "He was wounded for our transgressions (sins) He was bruised for our iniquities (sickness and diseases) Surely He bore our sorrows (hurts, discouragement's, etc.) And by His stripes we are healed." Jesus did it all for you. Nothing is impossible with God! He loves you. He wants to do what is best for you. Sometimes we may have to suffer for His sake. Praise God for that because He's shaping us and molding us and making us ready to enter into His Kingdom, to be with Him!

Dear Heavenly Father, I ask a special anointing on these WORDS that Your healing power be manifested to those who read or hear them. May Your healing hand be upon them and may they be filled to overflowing with Your precious Holy Spirit. May they be filled with Your love, Your peace, and Your joy. In the name of Jesus Christ of Nazareth! Amen.

IS YOUR HEART CLUTTERED

Today you constantly hear warnings about keeping your cholesterol level low. We are told there is a good and a bad cholesterol. The bad consists of fatty substances that cling onto one another and keep building until they block the flow of blood in the arteries to the heart. This can lead to a heart attack and possibly death. Thank God there are people who care enough to warn us of this possible hindrance to our lives and help enlighten and encourage us as to how to deal with the problem. We can be saved from a lot of pain and anguish by changing our eating habits, exercising and following our doctor's advice.

Are you aware that even if your cholesterol level is very low you can still have a problem with your heart? Just like your physical heart, your spiritual heart can get cluttered and/or totally blocked and hinder the flow of the Holy Spirit in our lives. The substances or attitudes that can cling together and build on one another could be un-forgiveness, negativeness, disobedience, pride, lying, fault-finding, jealousy, murmuring, bitterness, back-biting, selfishness, resentment, stubborness, un-teachableness, un-love, bickering, etc. They all add up to block the flow. This can lead to loss of joy, hope and peace. It can also lead to spiritual death.

How can you combat this spiritual heart trouble? Exercise . . . recognize what you are doing . . . . Bend your knee . . . Bow down before the Lord Jesus Christ and ask His forgiveness for your attitude . . . your cluttered condition. Lay all the problems at His feet and ask Him to be Lord of the situation and to cleanse you from all un-righteousness . . . and *allow His will* to be done . . . not yours. Change your eating habits . . . Feed on His Word, (the Bible), to help keep you strong in Him. Heed the advice of the Great Physician . . . Dr. Jesus, who will help us to keep the debris from coming in and if it does happen to get in, will show us how to break it up and get rid of it right away so that it cannot silently grow bigger and bigger and block the flow of the precious Holy Spirit in our lives without us being aware.

Why not take a few minutes now to take inventory. Is your spiritual heart in need of a little cleaning? Ask the Lord Jesus to light up the darkness in the very corners of your heart, so that the pathway is clear and safe and you won't stumble and fall. Don't put it off . . . . DO IT NOW, before it is too late.

IS THERE A LOVER IN YOUR HOUSE?

When a man wants to meet a woman he looks for a way to be introduced so they can get to know each other. He woos her, he calls her and talks to her, asks her out, compliments her, does nice things for her. He shows his love in many ways to win her affection. He usually wants her to love him, to be a companion, to share things with him, to be supportive and positive, trusting and doing nice things for him.

Well, GOD IS LOVE. He sent His Son, Jesus in the flesh to die on the cross for our sin. He rose from the dead so that we may have an advocate before the Father that we may be reconciled with Him. Then when Jesus went to be with the Father, He said He would send the Comforter, the Holy Spirit.

The Holy Spirit in His ministry woos us with all love, trying to show us the way to Jesus. Revealing to us how we can be put right with God the Father. He calls you, He does nice things for you. He shows you He's there in so many ways.

Just like with man or woman, you do not have to accept the wooing. You can turn down or discourage them or tell them NO, so also, with the Holy Spirit, you do not have to accept the call to love through Jesus Christ. But, if you do, there are many gifts and fruits and joys as well as hardships as you grow together.

You are assured, through letting Jesus be Lord of your life, that you have Jesus' love in you, through the Holy Spirit. By asking Jesus to forgive your sins and come into your heart, your body becomes the temple of the Holy Spirit. Then you really will have a lover in your house, and He will never leave you nor forsake you. You will be loved by Him. He'll be your companion. He'll talk with you, uplift you, listen to you and you will be with Him for eternity.

THANKFUL FOR A CHANGE

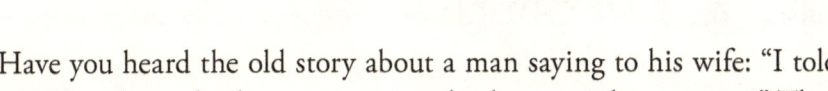

Have you heard the old story about a man saying to his wife: "I told you I loved you the day we got married, what more do you want?" They had been married 40 years. You may snicker at this statement but it is really sad when you think about it.

Isn't that basically what we tell God sometimes? Once we commit our lives to the Lord, Jesus Christ, we sometimes get to a place where we are doing things for the Lord through the church and end up doing things to the church as a body. For instance, we spend most of our life in a church, we spend our time and talents and continually make decisions how it should be run . . . one way . . . our way. When changes are needed to help a dying or dormant church to grow and be vital again for the Lord, we can't vision the spiritual because we are so hung up in the physical: "Well, this is the way it's always been done and that is the way it will stay!" You must always say No, or complain about any change especially if something might have changed without your knowledge.

Jesus came to change things . . . . shake things up! He sure shook up the Pharisees . . . . (Everything right and proper the way it's always been.) They were the last word on rules and regulations. Then there were the Saducces who could not look past the cross. They helped drive the nails in Jesus' hands as they could not see past their own views to see Jesus clearly. They did not want to change their minds to follow Him. Jesus showed them the way, right where they were but they decided No and complained a lot.

We should all be thankful that we are allowed to change at times. To just be open to change sometimes helps us to think more clearly. Are we, you and I, tying God's hands in our church, our neighborhood, our friends, our families, our lives? Will we allow the Holy Spirit to move and to guide, so that we, as the Body of Christ, are doing His will, not our own.

Thank you, Father, for your Son, Jesus and for your Holy Spirit. Thank you for changing me. Do I need another change? Please show me and cleanse me from all unrighteousness. Help me to do Your will, not mine, so that YOUR CHURCH will grow, spiritually and physically in Jesus' Name. AMEN

WHAT VISION!

There is much speculation about the Madonna figure etched in a rainbow of color in the glass of the Seminole Finance Building on the corner of US 19 and Drew Streets in Clearwater, Florida.

Could this be of God? Is it a miracle? The rainbow coloring is in other glass on the building, but only one Madonna figure is cast.

OK, something, (scientific, if you like), caused the rainbow effect coloring in the glass—wind, rain, sand, pollution, whatever. What are the odds of it creating a Madonna figure, and only one, that is outstanding?

Is God speaking to us? Trying to get our attention? People always seem to be looking for signs or a point of hope. Is this a point of hope for you?

The rainbow was given as a sign of the promise or covenant between God and man and every living creature on earth. A reminder, that He would never again destroy everything on earth by a flood. Genesis 9:11-17

Maybe through the rainbow etched glass we could reflect on His promise of a Savior, a baby born of a virgin, God's Son, who is no longer a babe, but who was crucified, died and was resurrected and now sits at the right hand of God, as a reminder. He died for you and wants to have fellowship with you.

Maybe, this is a way, to remind people of Jesus' birth because the "nativity scenes" are no longer allowed to be put up on Federal buildings. "The stones shall cry out . . . the Glory of God!" Luke 19:37-40.

Let's see, sand is made from stones . . . glass is made from sand and a rainbow is a sign of God's promise or covenant.

Interesting, isn't it?

God's ways are higher than our ways! Who knows the mind of God? Different things have different meanings to each individual. Is this your touch point? Is God touching your heart with hope?

As you rush to and fro, whether shopping, going to work, or school, and you drive by, or see a picture or hear someone talking about the rainbow etched Madonna figure . . . why not stop and reflect on Jesus and His love for you. Open your spiritual eyes and ears and then open your heart to God. Is He waiting to speak to you? Will you listen?

In the Bible, God used a donkey to save Baalam from destruction. Is this His way of saving you?

Does He have a vision for you? He sure does! Is this of God? Ask Him! Then listen . . . Want to learn more? Read the Gospel of John, Chapters 14, 15, 16, and 17. Also the 20th chapter verses 30 and 31. Then you decide what you want to believe!

WHAT CAN WE GIVE?

John 3:27
"No one can have anything unless
God gives it to him".

All of John Chapter 3 is very special to me. This particular book of the Bible enabled me to understand what the Lord wanted from me. I would like to share this experience with you.

After many years of thinking I was a "good" Christian, I found out I really didn't know what a real Christian was. But, Praise the Lord, I do now! What the Lord wanted from me was so simple, but all those years I couldn't see it.

He just wanted me to talk to Him. By myself . . . . Just Jesus and me. I told Him I knew He died on the cross for my sins. I knew I was a sinner and asked Him to forgive me. Then, most importantly, I asked Him to come into my heart and mold me into the person He wants me to be.

I committed my life totally to Christ . . . . no reservations. I was born again and my life has drastically changed. I was a very nervous person . . . . not now! I smoked . . . . not now! I swore at times . . . not now! Had no confidence . . . . now all my confidence is in the Lord Jesus Christ! Why these changes in my life? I didn't do it. I couldn't!

The Lord did it! He is working in me through the Holy Spirit and changing my life. It takes time. I still have my ups and downs but when I look to the Lord for His help and guidance, He's always there.

"He stands at the door and knocks". That is the door to your heart. YOU must invite Jesus in.

Footnote: Mother's day is this month so thought I'd share the message I gave at a Mother-Daughter Banquet a few years ago. What could be more important to pass on to our daughters than the knowledge of how to be born again, accept Jesus as Lord and Savior of their life so that they may receive eternal life through Him. Praise the Lord, my daughters are born again. Are yours? Are you?

May the Lord Jesus touch your body, mind and spirit with His healing love through the power of the precious Holy Spirit. May He make a way where there is no way for a positive improvement in your heart and life. In Jesus' Name! Amen.

CHECK YOUR GIFTS

Are you a young couple that the Lord might be speaking to that could use your gifts to help work with the youth of our church?

Do you have a musical gift that can be used for the Glory of God. Do you play a musical instrument? Are you gifted in song that you might sing unto the Lord? Is it drama or writing or directing?

How about the gift of helps . . . is that one of yours? Can you clean, mend, hammer, saw, paint, type, file, answer phones, make phone calls, rake, mow, cook, do electrical work, masonry, plumbing, lay tiles, carpet, use the computer, be an usher or greeter, and /or pray?

Do you have the gift of teaching? Either adults or youth or in the nursery. Has God given you insight to His Word and the ability to allow the Holy Spirit to teach through you?

Are you using your gift? Let Pastor know if God is speaking to you about a way you can serve. Don't let your gift get rusty. If you are not sure of your gift, let someone help you discover what God has for you. If you have accepted Jesus as your Lord and Savior, you do have a gift or gifts that God has given you. He gives good gifts to His children.

Every Christian is a vital part of the Body of Christ, working together for His Glory. Are you using your gifts or talents God has given you for the benefit of the Whole Body? YOU . . . CAN MAKE A DIFFERENCE!!!

JESUS IS THE LIGHT

Jesus is the Light—Jesus in us, is the Light in us. He makes us fishers of men. Let your light shine so others can see and men and women will come to the Light (Jesus in you).

Jesus says: "I am the Light of the world." "Whoever follows Me will never walk in darkness." John 8:12

Simon Peter said to the other disciples "I am going fishing." "We will come with you." They told Him. So they went out in a boat, but all that night they did not catch a thing. As the sun was rising, Jesus stood at the water's edge, but the disciples did not know that it was Jesus. Then He asked them, "Young men, haven't you caught anything?"

"Not a thing," they answered. He said to them "Throw your net out on the right side of the boat, and you will catch some." So they threw the net out and could not pull it back in, because they had caught so many fish. John 21:3-6

Jesus (the Light), appeared to the disciples. If we follow "The Word" . . . ."The Light", JESUS, and let Him have every part of our lives we would radiate with His Light . . . for each part we give to Him adds a little more Light within to shine through us. If we follow "The Light" . . . . "The Word", JESUS, and allow Him to lead, then many fish will be in the net . . . . full to overflowing!

Before the world was created, The Word already existed; He was with God, and He was the same as God. From the very beginning the Word was with God. Through Him, God made all things; not one thing in all creation was made without Him. The Word was the source of life, and this life brought Light to mankind. The Light shines in the darkness, and the darkness has never put it out.

God sent His messenger, a man named John, who came to tell people about the Light, so that all should hear the message and believe. He himself was not the Light; he came to tell about the Light. This was the real Light . . . the Light that comes into the world and shines on all mankind.

The Word was in the world, and though God made the world through Him, yet the world did not recognize Him. He came to His own country, but His own people did not receive Him. Some, however, did receive Him and believed in Him; so He gave them the right to become God's children. They did not become God's children by natural means, that is by being born as the children of a human father; God Himself was their Father.

The Word became a human being full of grace and truth, and lived among us. We saw His glory, the glory which He received as the Father's only Son. John 1:1-14.

Jesus said in a loud voice, "Whoever believes in Me believes not only in Me but also in Him who sent Me. I have come into the world as light, so that anyone who believes in Me should not remain in the darkness. If anyone hears My message and does not obey it, I will not judge Him. I came not to judge the world, but to save it. Whoever rejects Me and does not accept My message has one who will judge him. The words I have spoken will be his judge on the last day! This is true, because I have not spoken on My own authority, but the Father who sent Me has commanded Me what I must say and speak. And I know that His command brings eternal life. What I say, then, is what the Father has told Me to say." John 12:44-50

Jesus is calling you, yes, YOU! Have you responded? Will you step out and stand up for Jesus? He said "Acknowledge Me before men and I will acknowledge you before My father in heaven." "No one can come to the Father except by Me." John 14:6

Let today be your Heavenly Father's Day . . . . Ask Him to forgive you of your sin and cleanse you from all unrighteousness . . . and ask Him to be Lord of your life . . . and become a child of the Most High God!! Do it now . . . you will be so glad you did, for Jesus loves you so much and wants you to have a personal relationship with Him and

His Father . . . who will then be your Father. Then tell someone what you've done and let them share the joy with you. Then you will sing with joy "I'm so glad I'm a part of the Family of God . . . I've been washed in the fountain, cleansed by His blood! Joint heirs with Jesus as we travel this sod, For I'm part of the family, the Family of God.

WAR IS ENDED . . . .

No, it has to continue . . . that is . . . Our war as Christians with powers and principalities and rulers of darkness.

We have to continue as warriors in prayer. As, I believe, it is only by the prayers of the people that we had such an astounding victory with so few casualties in Desert Storm. Just think about it . . . . It is a MIRACLE with all those thousands of troops and weapons out there, so very few were lost. That is ONLY BY THE GRACE OF GOD! Woe be unto us, the United States of America, if we turn our backs or just be passive about communing with God each and every day. We must go to Him, on our knees, and fervently pray for our families, friends, country, allies, and the world, that they may come to know Jesus Christ as their Lord and Savior, and then and only then will the war be ended.

The Bible says: "That if thou shalt confess with thy mouth the Lord Jesus, and shalt believe in thine heart that God hath raised Him from the dead, thou shalt be saved. For with the heart, man (or woman or child), believeth unto righteousness, and with the mouth confession is made unto salvation." Romans 10:9,10 Have you done it? Did you tell someone about it? If not, why not do it NOW! Then, you too, can have the assurance of knowing that . . . . IN THE END . . . WE WIN!! HALLELUJAH!! WE WIN!!

INDEPENDENCE DAY—JULY 4TH

In our country, this is a very important date we celebrate, especially with all that is happening in the world today. God has really blessed us so much in this country but we, at one time or another over the years, have lost bits and pieces of the values and commitments that were evident when Independence was declared in this country on July 4th, 1776.

Why? How? What can we do? Maybe it was because of not wanting to get involved or thinking how could one person or only a few make a difference or that it was inevitable . . . why bother? Were some afraid of what others might think or that speaking out for God or Christian principles would jeopardize their jobs or their friends and possibly even their families? Were they lulled into thinking there were enough people who thought the way they did . . . those people would take care of it, they didn't really need their input? The tragic reality is there weren't enough who stood up and said "NO . . . you can't change what was fought so hard to achieve for the people of our country who are God-fearing and God-loving men and women!" Thus, many important laws were changed and most of God's laws and principles were taken out. Men and women gave their lives that we be one nation under God and that we be free. They had made a total commitment to God and country. Without God, there is no freedom.

How far we have come from that day . . . . Are you afraid to stand up for what is right? Have you lost a lot of your freedom? At home, at work, in your neighborhood, your church, your community, your state, and/or in your great country, the United States of America . . . . One nation, under God????

LET FREEDOM RING!! You and I can do it today . . . now . . . it is so simple we tend to overlook what is needed. A commitment to

God is first. God, please forgive me for all that I have done to offend you. Thank you that you sent your Son, Jesus to die on the cross for my sin, so that I may have a personal relationship with you. Come into my heart, Jesus, and be Lord of my life. Thank you for dying for my sin and that you rose from the dead and sent us the comforter, the Holy Spirit to guide us in all Truth. Show me the Truth, Lord. Show me what you would have me do, so that I will have your freedom in my heart, my home, at work, school, play, my neighborhood, church, community, state and country.

Use us, give us wisdom and knowledge to know how we can return, to one nation under God. Teach us to pray and turn from our wicked ways . . .

IN JESUS'S NAME . . . . LET FREEDOM RING . . . . IN OUR COUNTRY . . . . IN OUR HEARTS AND IN OUR SPIRITS . . . . AMEN.

THERE IS JOY IN THE LORD

The joy that Jesus gives me is overwhelming. He leads me through the Holy Spirit to the life He has set aside for me. At times, my patience is tested but if I stand and wait for His guidance then I have the joy and peace of knowing I am doing what He wants.

Guide me, Lord, for your plan for the ministry you want me to follow. Grant me the wisdom to know and listen when You speak to me through the Holy Spirit. My life is Yours. My will is Yours, I am ready to do whatever's asked of me. Please let me hear Your directions as to the path You want me to take. Most glorious Lord, I am completely Yours to do Your will. Lead me, Lord. I am willing, with my heart full of love for You. Your love filling my heart and working within me by the power of the Holy Spirit that I may be able to help others find You, and accept you as their Lord and Savior and then be blessed by the Holy Spirit. I humbly ask that You may grant me all or as many gifts of the Holy Spirit You desire me to have and that I may use them to glorify You, Lord. You know I speak from my heart, as my love for You is so great. Help me to keep the evil one out of my life so that I may work only for You and Your glory. Please forgive me for any wrongs I might do as I don't always realize what I do that may be wrong in Your eyes. Forgive me, Lord and help me to see the errors of my ways and repent or make right what I have messed up. My most merciful and mighty Lord and Savior, I cannot praise You enough. Thank you, Jesus, for I am richly blessed to be a child of Yours. Thank you for the joy and peace You have given me. I await Your call to do Your will.

GOD'S PROMISE

Just the other day two answers to prayer had been shared with me . . . 'twas a gloomy day and raining . . . . when all of a sudden I saw the sun was shining . . . All I could think of at that moment was . . . a rainbow . . . . there must be a rainbow . . . . God promised! I went out my back door . . . nothing . . . . I ran through the house and out the front door and sure enough . . . there it was!! A Big Beautiful Rainbow! It was a double rainbow . . . . the bottom was beautiful vivid colors . . . the middle was filled with dark clouds . . . then there was another arch of vivid colors shining over the dark clouds. It was breathtaking! I ran into the house to get my camera asking God to let me capture His beauty on film . . . . As I was taking the pictures I could almost hear God saying, "See, I keep My promises!" "I'll always keep My promises!" Hallelujah! He sure does! Look to Him . . . His Word is TRUE . . . His joy complete!

ARE YOU SLEEPING?

As the days of fall begin, and the weather turns a bit nippy in the morning, it gets a bit tougher to get out from under the covers and leave the warmth and comfort of the bed . . . . doesn't it? Feels so good we have to make an extra effort to get up and do the things we should be doing.

Are you too comfortable spiritually? Have you been under the covers . . . so to speak . . . regarding your walk with God? Isn't it time you extended some extra effort to get up and get going for His sake before it's too late?

God gave His Son, Jesus, to die for us . . . the least we can do is stand up for Him and follow His example, which is found in His Word, the Bible. If we confess Him before men, He will confess us before His Father in heaven.

Time to do some fall housecleaning . . . dust off your bibles and your knees and your voices so that your prayers, praise, and thanksgiving can flow freely to the throne. Ask the Holy Spirit to be renewed in you to fill you to overflowing. Set Him free to work in your life. Throw off the covers . . . and join the Body of Christ . . . . Renewed and Revitalized . . . to do His will, not ours.

Are you sleeping? Are you sleeping? Brother John? . . . Sister Sue? WAKE UP! WAKE UP! Your redemption draweth nigh . . . . Jesus is coming soon . . . . Are you ready? Make that extra effort . . . . Go to the altar . . . Seek Him and ye shall find. Christians fight on their knees! And we win! Hallelujah WE WIN!

CLEANING OUT

While getting our house ready to be put on the market we'd clean or paint and finish the room or portion we were doing and say "looks good"! Then a few hours or a few days later you happen to see you missed a spot or there was something that needed tending to that you never even saw before. Just when you think you are all finished . . . no more to do . . . a light bulb burns out or a door sticks or squeaks. A house needs constant care, cleaning and evaluation.

I couldn't help but think that is the way with our walk with the Lord . . . after our initial commitment the Holy Spirit helps us to clean up our life and just when we think we're "looking good" spiritually, the Holy Spirit humbles us a bit and shows us He's not finished with us yet. We still have spots here and there we missed or we get tired and forget about reading the Word and our light begins to dim. We may also get stuck as we continue to do things our way and not His. We may also squeak by complaining or talking about how others are living their lives, instead of evaluating how we are living and keeping our mind, body and spirit clean before our Father in heaven through His Son, Jesus, who set us free with the help of the Holy Spirit whom enables us to be more like Jesus. Think about it . . . then strive to do what needs to be done to get your house in spiritual order. Me too. Amen? Amen!!

ARE YOU FILLED?

Around Thanksgiving time we are reminded of the "Love Feast" of the past, when the Pilgrims and Indians came together to celebrate the harvest and to Thank God for all that He had provided for them. Here the two quite opposite groups came together in one accord . . . . forgetting their differences . . . Each giving the fruit of their labors, their individual personalities, products of their culture and themselves. Each receiving due to their giving. They at least for this event accepted each other as they were.

If only that same spirit had prevailed instead of each one coming to the place where they wanted everything their way and ended up with a TAKE . . . TAKE . . . TAKE attitude and little if any GIVE. Many died needlessly because of this fact.

You and I come together on Sundays, each bringing our past experiences with us along with our present lifestyles and beliefs and the fruit of our labor. We come to thank God and Praise and Worship Him because of who He is and because He sent Jesus—in our place—to that cross on Calvary and Jesus took our sin upon Himself and died . . . . So that we could be reconciled to the Father. Three days later, He rose from the dead but before He ascended He said He'd send us the Comforter. The Holy Spirit, to guide us and teach us what we need to know, to live as God would have us live.

Even though we all come from different backgrounds, denominations, races, cultures and social classes, we should be coming together as the Body of Christ for one reason . . . To give thanks and praise, and worship the Lord our God for who He is and what He and His Son, Jesus, have done for us.

A question to ask ourselves is this: Do we come to church or approach God to give or to get? Haven't we already gotten? We have our homes . . . protection from weather, food to eat, clothes to wear, air to breathe, freedom to do almost anything. Isn't it time, that when we come together and approach our Wonderful God, that we give to Him? What would God want from us? . . . . you ask. Obedience . . . He'd like us to use the gift He promised He'd send. Ourselves . . . Each day we should ask the Holy Spirit to enlighten our minds and pray for the Pastor that the Lord will reveal to him what He wants to tell us through him. Also that we be open to His leading by inviting the Holy Spirit to discipline us, mold us and shape us into Jesus' disciples . . . that we may do His will, not ours. One very important thing we can do also, is to accept other people or Christians as they are, just as Jesus accepts us just the way we are . . . . focus on asking the Holy Spirit to change us, and let God take care of changing others.

Someone told me once . . . you have to give to get . . . spiritually speaking. You can't buy it and you can't earn it!

For example: If you had a glass of water . . . filled to the brim . . . you couldn't receive any more into the glass unless some was poured out. Then, and only then, could the glass receive more. If you never changed the water by pouring some out and putting fresh in, the water would become stagnant.

We are God's vessels. Do we keep the Living Water to ourselves and become stagnant? Or, Do we give out the Spirit in praise and worship and thanksgiving, allowing Him to flow in our lives . . . thus, giving Him room. He will not force His way in or out. You hold the key to the door. The key to releasing and refilling is praise and worship . . . inviting the Holy Spirit to have His way, not our way.

R U filled? Or, are you dying needlessly, by becoming stagnant? It's beginning to rain . . . . Will you bend at the knee and let praise and thanksgiving pour out to God so that the Holy Spirit can flow in and through you and keep you fresh as a mountain stream? Just remember . . . you can't out give God. Release some praises, and thanksgiving and worship God . . . then ask, "Fill my cup, Lord . . . I lift it up, Lord . . . Come, and quench this yearning of my soul. Bread of Heaven feed me till I want no more . . . Fill my cup, Fill it up, and MAKE ME WHOLE!!!! HE WILL!!!!

Dear Heavenly Father,

Thank you, Lord, and Praise Your Holy Name. You are so worthy of being praised. Your LOVE for us abounds and we are ever mindful, especially during the Christmas Holiday Season that you love us so much, You sent Your Son, Jesus, in human form and He was born of a virgin, in a manger. He experienced all the things that are common unto man but did not sin. He took our sin upon Himself. He was the Lamb that was slain . . . . crucified, died and buried . . . but then . . . He rose again, victor over sin and death. He made the way for us to be put right with you, Father. For if we go to Jesus and commit our life to Him, and are sincerely sorry for our sins and ask Him to forgive us, then we are forgiven. Thank you, Father for making the way.

Lord, Your Word says, "Ask anything in My Name, believing, and ye shall receive!" I stand on your promise now that each person reading this will have a special touch from You of healing in their body, mind and spirit. May those that don't know You in a personal way open their heart to accept Jesus as their Lord and Savior and those who have strayed to re-commit their lives to You and feel Your overwhelming love and peace.

Let this Christmas be a Miracle Christmas for each one. In Jesus' Name. Amen!

IT'S FREE

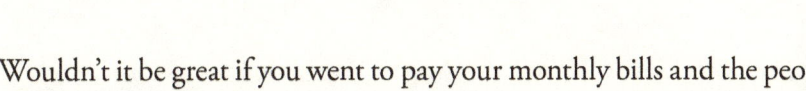

Wouldn't it be great if you went to pay your monthly bills and the people said to you . . . . Someone has already paid for them! What would you do? Would you try find out more about that person? Tell others? Thank this person? Thank God for this person? Speak good of this person?

Do you know that Jesus Christ paid the price for your sins? Do you know that He went to the cross and took your sins upon Himself, willingly? Did you know God sent His Son, Jesus, to die in your place so that you might have salvation . . . Eternal Life with Him? Well, He did it for you, as a free gift, because He loves you. He accepts you just the way you are no matter what you look like, no matter what you have done. All you have to do is: Ask Him to forgive your sins and repent (turn away from those sins) and ask Him what He would have you do . . . . and follow Him. Sincerely ask Him to come into your heart and life and that He be truly Lord of your life from this day forward. Then what do you do? Find out more about Him! Read the Bible . . . start with the New Testament . . . at least a chapter a day. Tell others about Him! What He has done for you and what He'll do for them. Thank Jesus for what He's done. Thank God for sending Him. Praise Him! For the only way to the Father is through His Son, Jesus.

Rejoice! He lives! . . . . and He wants to live inside you. Ask Him in today . . . it's a life-changing experience.

"Listen! I stand at the door and knock; if anyone hears my voice and opens the door, I will come in to Him, and will sup with Him, and He with me." (Revelation 3:20)

PRAYER

May the Lord Jesus, the Christ, Son of the Living God, touch each of you with His healing power . . . from the very top of your head to the very tips of your toes. May He continue to renew your mind and may you renew your commitment to Him during this glorious celebration of His birth. Then may He fill you to overflowing with the Holy Spirit that you may walk with Him and talk to Him as He brings you through any problem you may encounter in your lifetime. In Jesus' Name . . . AMEN.

O COME, LET US ADORE HIM, CHRIST THE LORD!

How can we adore Him? First of all, what does adore mean? Well, let's see . . . . I have my trusty dictionary right here . . . adore . . . here it is! 1. to worship or honor as a deity or as divine. 2. to regard with reverent admiration and devotion. 3. to be extremely fond of . . . also see revere. Looking under revere, at the end of various definitions it states: ADORE implies love and stresses the notion of an individual and personal attachment.

How can you be fond of, worship, honor, regard with reverent admiration and devotion, love, and have a personal attachment to someone you don't really know? Do you know Jesus well enough? If you don't, do you want to? Seek Jesus out . . . ask Him to reveal Himself to you. Jesus IS the ANSWER . . . . HE is the reason for the season! He loves you and wants to welcome you with open arms into His family. Do you think you've done something so bad that He would never forgive you? You haven't, for if you come to Him sorry for what you have done and wanting Him to help change you . . . He will not turn you away. All you have to do is ask, believing, and you shall receive!

GREAT IS THE LORD . . . AND GREATLY TO BE PRAISED!! HALLELUJAH!

THOUGHTS AT CHRISTMAS

During the holiday season so many things to do! Shopping, wrapping, baking, trimming . . . . seems like no end in sight! Amidst all the clamor and excitement of this season however, many thoughts come to mind. What are we celebrating? A child was born, a very precious child, who is our Savior and Lord. This miraculous event occurred many, many years ago, but even to this day is most meaningful to all. Yes, Christmas has been commercialized in many ways—but—does this make a difference or should it make a difference about our personal feelings of Christmas and the birth of Jesus? It can't make a difference as long as we remember the true meaning and our hearts are full of love. Love of Christ and our fellow man.

Who or what is Santa? How do you look at it? Here is where the difference may lie. He is a symbol, maybe, for what, of what? Well, when you stop and think about Santa, don't you think about giving? The giving and sharing of gifts, food, time, money and love, which brings happiness and joy to those around you. Isn't this somewhat similar to what the Wise Men did when Christ was born? Isn't it through Christ's love that we are able to do these things and enable "Santa" to be? A tool in witnessing, to bring fuller understanding of what giving and sharing of yourself and what is yours is, so that we may extend ourselves and be ever so thankful to our Lord for all that He does, is doing and shall do for all mankind. Only He can be our life, our salvation, our peace. Give thanks unto Him!

May His light shine upon you and grant you peace and understanding for a blessed Christmas and may He light your life for a most meaningful New Year!

LETTER FROM SANTA

Dear

Ho! Ho! Ho! So good to be able to share with you a few things that happened this year. Thanks for thinking of me. I really appreciate your friendship.

We at the North Pole have been on an exercise program to keep us healthy and in good shape. Although we get more exercise laughing and helping others get on their feet and out of things than exercising.

Did you ever see reindeer try to stand on their back legs and touch their toes with their front hooves? Oh, Ho, Ho, my belly aches every time I picture it! They fall over sideways in the snow . . . . PLOP!

Did you ever watch an elf jog in the deep snow? Hee, Hee, now you see them, now you don't! They have to write their names down before they leave so we can find them. They always run where the deer had made tracks with their hooves in the snow and Whoosh! . . . they'd fall right into the holes. Then, they would get laughing so hard they couldn't get out. We giggle every time we think about it.

It is a great gift to be able to laugh at yourself. Did you ever feel all alone and that no one really cares about you? Or understands? Because I look different with my big tummy and my red suit and black boots people chuckle when they see me. When my tummy shakes they really laugh. I couldn't laugh at myself because I couldn't see myself as other people did, but now I know I really do look funny sometimes.

Really, I was never very happy until I met the best friend anyone could ever have. His name is Jesus, He's the Son of the Living God. Since Jesus came into my heart I can laugh at my tummy, especially when it jiggles like jello!

Did you know you could have eternal life? That Jesus died for you?

Yes, He loves you that much! After three days He rose from the dead and proved He had power over death, sin, sickness and the devil. He is alive, right now, and wants you to invite Him into your life to be your Savior and friend.

That is why we celebrate Christmas. It is the birthday of Jesus. You usually aren't invited to a Birthday Party if you don't know that person. But Jesus knows and loves you. That's why He died, to know you and invite you to His Birthday Party.

Would you like to have Jesus as your friend, Lord, and Savior? You'll be part of God's family for Christmas and for eternity! You know, you are very special to Him. He loves you just the way you are.

If you are sorry for your sins . . . like lying, talking bad to anyone, fighting, taking something that doesn't belong to you, tell Jesus and ask Him to come into your heart and be Lord of your life. He will never leave you nor forsake you. He will be inside you always, to help you. If you do ask Him in, will you write and let me know so I can share your happiness? Tell me if you have a Bible so you can read the letters that Matthew, Mark, Luke and John wrote to help you learn more about Jesus and how He wants you to live.

JESUS LOVES YOU SO DO I,

Santa

P.S. Got to go now and finish packing the sleigh. I also have to round up the reindeer to do their warm up exercises before we go.

EGGS?

While I was sitting waiting for some eggs to boil for egg salad, the Lord gave me quite a revelation about the Trinity—The Holy Trinity. I would like to share that revelation with you:

The Lord said an egg is like God. He said to take the complete egg, the shell, the yolk, and the white part. When all together in one, that's God—that's the Sovereign God. Picture that egg as God surrounding us. His people sinned. God had made a covenant that people could have their sins forgiven by sacrifice. The animal that they sacrificed has to be pure, with no blemish. Well, God revealed to me that because people sinned, He needed a perfect sacrifice for the forgiveness of sins—to take them away once and for all. He knew the only perfect sacrifice would be if part of Him was sent in the flesh to be sacrificed.

So the shell opened and from within that shell came the yolk. Now, think about the yolk of the egg. The yolk is round and yellow. When you think of it and look at it, it can represent the sun. Well, that reminds us of His Son, Jesus Christ. The yellow part of an egg is the seed, as it were, for the little chicks that are born from the egg. It is a reminder of life because that's where the life comes from—the yolk, the little chick, the seed. And so God took that seed and placed it into a virgin and He allowed that seed, part of Himself, to be born into human form, to take on our human nature, to be inside that human being. And it was a human being, but yet it was God. And His name was Jesus. And that is where life—eternal life—comes from—Jesus.

As Jesus grew and learned, He was without blemish. There was no sin in Him. He was the only perfect being, free of any sin. But, He had a mission, being the only perfect sacrifice, He had to lay down His life for your sin, and my sin. Which was what He did, willingly.

He laid down His life for YOU! He went to that cross and He took every sin, every sickness and disease upon Himself. He was wounded for our transgressions. He was bruised for our iniquities. Surely, He bore our sorrows. He took it all upon Himself and went to that cross for the forgiveness of our sin and by His stripes, we are healed. Praise God! After three days, He arose. When He ascended into heaven, He said to His apostles and His followers, "Wait, and I will send you a Comforter," and He did. He sent the Holy Spirit. That is what the white part of the egg represents—the Holy Spirit. Notice the white part of the egg, before it is cooked, it is transparent. But, you know it's there. You can't see the Holy Spirit. You can feel Him, you know He's there, but you can't see Him. Praise the Lord!

This is what the Trinity is—just like you can take an egg and you can open it, have the shell in one place, you can separate the yolk from the white part, as you do to make a cake, so that you have three separate things. You have the shell, the yolk, and the white (transparent) part of the egg. But, no matter which part you look at, it's still an egg. So, there's three in one, the Father, the Son, and the Holy Spirit; but they are all God—the Holy Trinity—God the Father, God the Son (Jesus Christ), and God the Holy Spirit; three separate persons, but one God.

A TRIBUTE TO DOROTHY BLOOM

———— ⁕ ————

While attending Bayside Community Church was felt led to start a prayer group several years ago. Had talked to Pastor Bates about it and he agreed it would be ok. I remember it was on a Tuesday morning and I was totally excited, anticipating what the Lord was going to do. I had made up a booklet with songs in them which I put on about 10 chairs . . . with the advertising in the bulletin I was hopeful. I waited and prayed and waited some more no one came . . . I asked the Lord why? I knew it was Him that had suggested this idea. Then I heard footsteps on the stairs . . . I breathed thank you, Lord and in walked this petite, bubbly, blonde lady who asked, "Is this the right place for the prayer group?" I said it sure is. We began talking and we both knew it was God who brought us together that particular day and it was by His design only the two of us would be there so we could get acquainted. We talked like we had known each other for years. We both loved the Lord with all our hearts, wanted to follow Him and do whatever He would have us do. We both agreed the Lord had led us to pray for the church. We had so many things in common in the Lord and in life we just bonded immediately. Since that day of beginnings we have had such a marvelous friendship!

Dorothy enriched my life in many ways . . . always so real, so caring, so loving and so in love with the Lord. Always giving her Lord credit for all He had done for her and the blessings she had in her wonderful caring husband, Jack and her very special children, grandchildren and siblings. All whom I have met or talked to are just so precious. What joy she experienced being with her family both near and far She loved the church and all her brothers and sisters there, always praying for them and helping wherever she could. She exuded the love of Jesus wherever she went to whomever she met. She was a hero, someone you could look up to as an example of how to live a Christian life. Dorothy trusted the Lord through her bout with breast cancer, her faith never wavered. She was always excited to share the Lord Jesus, what He has done in her life, that He was the answer. She always encouraged others to follow Him. Her greatest desire was that all of her family and all of her friends would have a personal relationship with Jesus.

Dorothy introduced me also to Aglow International (women's ministry) and we were privileged to go on a retreat together and what a glorious time we had in the Lord! She is a wonderful sister in the Lord; a cherished, faithful friend, whom I shall forever carry in my heart. Words cannot tell how spiritually uplifting our relationship was and how much of an impact she had on so very many. Praise you, Lord for allowing Dorothy to be a part of my life, I am richly blessed! I look forward to the day we will be reunited!

Shalom, Dorothy!

With Much Love, Serena

WORDS OF INSPIRATION
AND ENCOURAGEMENT

"Delight yourself in the Lord and
He will give you the desires of your heart." Psalm 37:4

My child, behold, the time is now
Time to reap and time to plow.
Time to hold you in Mine arms
So, My child, don't be alarmed.

My love for you forever grows, as I listen to your prayers.
When you worship at My feet, Mine eyes are wet with tears.
Be vigilant, My child, to always come to Me.
In trouble, joy or pondering, and sit upon My knee.

I long to have you visit and ask that you would stay.
Seek Me first, in all things, I will show the way.
My help, My love, My wisdom, to you I will impart.
Giving, always giving, from deep within My heart. 12/21/2008

My child,

You are My delight! I long to sup with you. I long to hear your voice.
I love you, child, with a deep abiding love. Come to Me all who are
weary and heavy laden and I shall give thee rest. My anointing is upon
you to go forth in My name to do My bidding. All is not as it seems,
I have gone before you. New doorways shall be opened unto you. Stay
close and I will show you when the time is right. Meanwhile, rest in
Me, allow Me to fill you to overflowing with My love, My peace and
My joy. I will pour you out blessings you will not have room to contain.
So much, that you will have to give away the overflow. Trust Me, child,
lean not to your own understanding. In all thy ways acknowledge Me
and I shall direct thy paths. By My stripes, you are healed! Embrace it!
Those whom I set free are free indeed.

01/02/2009

My child,

I am longing to hear your voice. It has been awhile since we have sat together. I miss you, child. I have much I want to say to you. I am here for you. I can help you through each day if you but put Me first in all things. I will guide you, I will walk before you. Lay your burdens at My feet all ye who are weary and heavy laden and I shall give you rest. Ask, and you shall receive, seek and you shall find, knock and the door shall be opened. My timing is perfect. Wait upon Me. Be patient, child, all shall work to the good. Trust Me, the answers will manifest soon. Trust Me, for I have you in the palm of My hand. Wait, therefore, upon the Lord and He shall deliver you. Be not discourage, your redemption draweth nigh.

01/11/2009

My child,

I have so much to tell you. Listen while I speak. Turn your heart toward Me. Allow Me room. Give Me first place in your life. Come to Me, all you that are weary and heavy laden and I shall give you rest. Seek Me in all things. I will show you the way. My ways are not your ways but My way is the best for you. I would that none should perish that all have eternal life with Me. There are those who will not listen. Seek Me with all your heart and lean not to your own understanding. In all your ways acknowledge Me and I shall direct your path. I have gone before you. I have opened doors that cannot be shut. I have given you many gifts to use for My glory. Do not step ahead, wait upon Me, for My timing is perfect. Be not anxious for what you will eat or drink for I shall supply all your needs. Trust Me, praise Me, for I alone am worthy to be praised. I love you, child, with a deep abiding love. Rest in Me and listen for My voice and Come, follow Me.

01/22/2009

My child,

I give My heart to you. I love you with a deep abiding love. I have not forgotten nor forsaken you. I am right here. I will never leave you nor forsake you. You are Mine, bought with a price. I have much in store for you. I shall provide all your needs. Be not dismayed, all will work together for good. There is much you do not understand but My way is best. Always seek My face, for I shall show you the path you must take that will fulfill all I have prepared before you. My ways are not your ways, child, but My ways are True. Seek Me first in all things and you shall see many wondrous things transpire around you. It is not by power, not by might but by My Spirit saith the Lord! I shall redeem you. You have been redeemed by the Blood of the Lamb. Go, therefore, and rejoice, your redemption draweth nigh.

02/04/2009

My child,

I have given you all that you need. You will succeed. Hold onto that which is good, throw off that which hinders your walk with Me. I have come that you have life and have it more abundantly. You are the apple of My eye. I long to gather you to Me as a hen gathers her chicks. Come to Me, all ye who are weary and heavy laden, I shall give you rest. Lean upon My breast as I speak many wondrous things. I have much to show you. Things are not always as they seem. Trust Me, for I am working. I am in control. All will work to the good. Be not dismayed for I have called you to this place at this time. Be thou diligent in thy love for Me. Let Me uphold you. Be not discouraged for soon you shall see the fruition of your labors. Many will come to Me because of your obedience. Be still and know that I am God, Jehovah. Stand fast, stand firm, for I am your All in All.

02/14/2009

My child,

My love for you is deep, never ending. I long to gather you to Me as a hen gathers her chicks. I long to speak to you. Come, sit with Me awhile, tell Me what you need. Let My love flow to you and through you. Feel My peace waft over you as you give all to Me. I shall relieve your burdens if you just give them to Me. Allow Me in child, I am here for you. I will never leave you nor forsake you. I do understand all you are going through. Trust Me, I shall supply all your needs. Be obedient to My Word and My ways and you shall see many answers come to pass. Lean on Me, child, I shall give you rest. Allow My Spirit to guide you and comfort you. Do not be dismayed for I have you in the palm of My hand and nothing or no one can snatch you from Me. Ask, believing, child and ye shall receive. Be not hasty, My timing is perfect. Wait for My leading.

02/26/2009
My child,
I am here for you. I have heard your cry. My heart goes out to you in your distress. I love you, child. I would never leave you nor forsake you. You are My beloved child. Have I not told you that you will see many things happen around you? I will get you through. Look to Me, lean on Me and I shall direct your path. You are Mine. No one can snatch you from Me. Come to Me all ye who are weak and heavy laden and I shall give you rest. Lay all at My feet and I shall lighten the load. Lean not to your own understanding but in all ways acknowledge Me and I shall direct your path. Be not dismayed for I will uphold you. Rest in Me, child. Seek not the favor of others. Follow Me, walk in My ways and you shall be delivered from that which oppresses you. Those whom I set free are free indeed. Keep your eyes on Me, child, I will show you the way. Behold, I stand at the door and knock. Open your heart to Me, child, let Me love you.

03/22/2009
My child,
You see what is before you. You know what My plan is for you in your very inner being. Seek Me, seek out the plan I have for you. Follow in My way and it shall be revealed. You are My delight! I long to sit with you and listen. I am here, child, look to Me. I do care about everything that happens in your life. I am always there for you. I shall protect you in the way I will show you. You are Mine, bought with a price, I will never leave you nor forsake you. You are My beloved child. Keep your eyes on Me. Do not go to the right or left, follow Me. My heart cries

for you. When you hurt, I hurt. I came that you have life and have it more abundantly. Do not be afraid to step out in faith. I will not let your foot dash upon a stone. I have all in control, trust Me, for I do not lie. I will uphold you with My right hand. Be still and know that I am God, Jehovah. Lean on Me, child, lean on Me. I am your Savior, your Deliverer, your Healer.

04/03/2009

My child,

I have given to you a new song. Sing out loud and clear. I will anoint you from on High to do My bidding. Many will be touched by your obedience. Go therefore, in My name, I shall uphold you. I will give you the words to say, My timing is perfect, child. I will prepare the way before you. I shall remove any hindrance. Be assured I have you in the palm of My hand. Nothing will be forgotten. All will come together for good. They will heed the call. Trust Me, for I shall draw all men unto Me. Be still and know that I am God. I am your Savior, Healer, Lord. Keep your eyes on Me and I shall direct your path. Be not dismayed for all that I have told you shall come to pass. Rest in Me, child, rest in Me.

04/13/2009

My child,

I love you deeply. You are My beloved child. Walk in My way. Listen to My voice for I have much to tell you. Be not dismayed at what is going on in the world for I have overcome the world. I am in control. I will show you the way in which I would have you go. Look to Me, seek Me first in all things and I shall direct your path. You are not alone. You are never alone. All will work to the good. Trust Me, I do not lie. I am the Alpha and Omega, the beginning and the end. I shall supply all your needs. Seek Me, read My Word, listen to My voice and Come, follow Me.

05/03/2009

My child,

I have given you the power to move mountains. I have given you all that you need to go forth and do My bidding. Lean on Me, for I am the Way, the Truth and the Light. No one can come to the Father except by Me. Hold fast to what you have been taught. Allow My Spirit to reveal to you what is in store. Trust Me. Lay all at My feet and I shall lift you up. Keep your eyes on Me. Let Me love you, child. Bask in My Presence for I shall grant you peace and wisdom and My love will flow to you and through you. Be ever vigilant to seek Me first in all things. You are My beloved child in whom I am well pleased.

05/18/2009

My child,

I have given all I have for you. You are My delight! Come, sit with Me. Tell Me all your heart's desires. I long to be with you. I long to hear your voice. There is so much going on in the world that is not of Me. But, trust Me, for I am in control. Many things shall come upon the earth that will make hearts feint. But, I am with you. Do not be afraid to go forth in My Name and do My bidding. Tell them, tell them of Me and My love. Be a witness unto Me that they might come to Me and bow their knee before Me. Tell them, before it is too late. I have given you all that you need. Go, therefore, and be a blessing. In all your ways acknowledge Me and I shall direct your path. Keep your eyes on Me, child, for I shall supply all your needs.

05/30/2009

My child,

Thank you for your love. My heart is full of love for you. I am delighted when you spend time with Me. I long to hear your voice as you speak to Me and tell Me what is on your mind. Leave all your burdens with Me, child, do not let them weigh you down. My yoke is easy, My burden light. Leave it all with Me and I shall lift you up. I shall set you free of all that hinders or binds you, if you will just give all to Me. I am your All in All. I shall set you free. I shall impart in you the peace that surpasses all understanding if you but look to Me in all things. Put Me first, child and trust Me, for I love you with a deep abiding love and I will never leave you nor forsake you. You are My beloved child. You will see many calamities. Do not worry or fret, for I am with you, I will protect you. You are Mine bought with a price. Lean on Me, child, lean not to your own understanding. In all your ways acknowledge Me and I shall direct your path. Behold, I come quickly in the twinkling of an eye. Be steadfast in Me. Keep your eyes on Me. Do not look to the right or to the left. I am God Jehovah.

06/09/2009
My child,
I hear your voice as you praise Me. I hear your prayers. My heart cries as I see all that is going on around you. Heed My Voice, turn to Me, for I am your Rock, I am your Fortress, I am your Deliverer. Trust Me, for I know the end from the beginning. Seek My face, turn from your wicked ways and I shall heal your land. Those who will not listen will suffer. Those who will not lay all at My feet will be lost. Tell them, tell them of Me and My love. I would that none should perish. Come to Me, all ye who are heavy laden and I shall give thee rest. Lay all at My feet and I shall lift you up. Seek Me, child, seek Me, and I shall impart to you wisdom and knowledge to know what I would have you do. Go therefore, in My Name and do My bidding. My anointing is upon you to heal the sick, to cast out demons. Stand firm in Me and be My ambassador. Keep your eyes on Me and I shall direct your path.

06/21/2009
My child,
I love thee with a deep abiding love. Stand firm in Me, for I have you in the palm of My hand. I will never leave you nor forsake you, child, for you are Mine, bought with a price. I gave My all for you and will continue to supply all your needs, if you but look to Me. Forgive those who mistreat you as I have forgiven you. Let My love flow to you and through you. My peace I give unto you. Be not worried or dismayed for I am with you. Go forth, child, in My Name and do My bidding. I

have anointed you from on High. Pray for one another that you shall be healed. Read My Word, Listen to My Voice and Come, follow Me. You are My beloved child in whom I am well pleased. You are My delight! Bask in My Presence, child, for I have called you by name. Be still and know that I am God, Jehovah Jirah, Your Provider.

06/22/2009
My child,
Take heart, child, for I am with you. I shall open doors that cannot be shut. Rest in Me, child, for I shall deliver you from all unrighteousness.

07/07/2009
My child,
I long to hear your voice. It warms My heart to see your love for Me. You are My delight. I long to enfold you in My arms and whisper in your ear many secrets I have in store for you. Listen, listen for My voice and follow My lead. I will show you the way in all things if you but look to Me and Me alone. For you are Mine bought with a price and I shall never leave you nor forsake you. You are My beloved child. Time grows short child, tell them of Me and My love. Let them know I await their call. I have provided the way. Trust Me, let Me show you the way you should go. You are My ambassador. Go therefore, in My Name, for I have anointed you from on High. Be ever faithful and put all in My hands and I shall lift you up. I shall open the door child, you must walk through.

07/21/2009
My child,
I long to caress your brow. I long to soothe your spirit. Allow Me access that I might take the burden from you. My yoke is easy, My burden light. Keep your eyes on Me, child. Allow Me to have free rein. I will show you the way I would have you go. I shall supply all your needs. Do not worry nor fret for I am in control. Open your heart, open your mind to Me. Many things will fall into place, just trust Me. I am your All in All. I have foreseen all that is going on around you. I will make

the way clear. I have given to you those that will uphold you. I have set all in motion. My ways are not your ways. My time is not your time but My way is better and My timing is perfect. Wait on Me, child, for the time grows short. Tell them of Me and My love and let My Spirit speak to their hearts. Come, follow Me.

07/24/2009
My child,

I have ordained you from on High to do My bidding. I shall supply all your needs. I will fill you to overflowing with My love, My peace, My joy, My wisdom. They will flow to you and through you. Keep your eyes on Me for I am your strength and shield. I am your All in All and I shall never fail you. I shall never forsake you. You are Mine, bought with a price. I love you, child, with a deep abiding love. Seek Me first, in all things and I shall lift you up. Rejoice, child, rejoice for your redemption draweth nigh. Let the anointing flow for I have deemed you righteous. Follow My lead, child and you shall see many wondrous events unfold before you for the mantle of My love and My Spirit are upon you. Go forth in victory for I am with you. Draw near to Me, sit upon My lap and let Me whisper in your ear the Love I have for you. I have called you to be My ambassador. Stand firm in Me and I shall direct your path. (Pastor Paul)

08/04/2009
My child,

I have given you all that you need to go forth and do My bidding. Seek My face, turn from your wicked ways and follow Me. You have asked, I have answered. Lay all at My feet. Let go of that which is hindering you. Read My Word, allow Me to speak to you. Open your heart and your mind to Me. Let not your heart be troubled. I have called you, do not doubt that. I will raise you up. Believe and you shall receive, My timing is perfect. All is being made ready, the door shall open soon. Walk through it confident that I have prepared the way before you. Praise Me, child. Worship Me in Spirit and in Truth. Keep your eyes on Me, do not look to the right nor the left. Come, follow Me!

08/16/2009

My child,

My heart cries out to you. There is so much anguish for My children. I love you with a deep abiding love. Stand fast, stand firm in Me, for I have you in the palm of My hand. I will never leave you or forsake you. Lay all at My feet, child. Let not your heart be troubled, I have much in store for you. Trust Me, for I shall bring you through. Hold on to that which is good and put off that which is evil. I have given you the power to move mountains. Go, therefore, in My Name and do My bidding. You are My beloved child. Come to Me . . . My yoke is easy, My burden light. Keep your eyes on Me and I shall direct your path. Come to Me, all ye who are weary and heavy laden and I shall give you rest.

08/31/2009

My child,

I have called you to this place. You have answered the call, therefore, I will bless you abundantly. I will go before you. I shall smite your enemies. You are one, in Me. You have fulfilled your vows and I shall lift you up. My hand is upon you, I have anointed you from on High to do My bidding. Go forth in Joy, knowing I am the God that healeth you. Go forth and minister in My Name for My Glory! I have given you many gifts, use them. Trust in Me, lay all at My feet. I will never leave you nor forsake you. My joy is full as you obey My Word and My way. Go forth in victory for I am with you. Those whom I set free are free indeed.

09/16/2009

My child,

I have seen all that goes on. I know your heart. Call upon Me and I shall answer you. Keep your eyes on Me, child, look not to the right nor the left. Do not worry about what men shall say. I have called you. Listen to My voice and follow Me. I have not given you a spirit of fear but of power and love and a sound mind. Go therefore, with confidence. Tell them of Me and My love. Look to Me, child, in all things. Trust Me to prepare the way before you. Lean on Me, for I am your All in All.

09/25/2009

My child,

I have given you much to ponder. Rely on Me, for I shall show you the way. I have many good things in store, if you but follow Me. You are My delight! I have not forsaken you. You shall see the manifestation of My love very soon. My power is within you and grows more and more as you look to Me in all things. Stand firm in Me. Let My love flow to you and through you as you minister in My Name. Peace be with you child. Things are not always as they seem. Look to Me in all things.

10/12/2009

My child,

I am giving you time to discern the situation, then I will show you what needs to be done. My ways are not your ways, but My way is best. All will fall into place for I shall go before you and prepare hearts. Let not your heart be troubled for I am with you. I have anointed you from on High for this purpose. Seek Me in all things. Listen, observe, then as I lead, act. Let My love flow to you and through you. Allow My Spirit free rein and many shall come to Me as Savior, Lord and Healer. My promises are True. Ask, believing and you shall receive. My love for you is deep, child. Lean thy head upon My breast and rest in Me, for I am with you always. Be still and know that I am God and My timing is perfect!

10/25/2009

My child,

I have everything in control Do not worry nor fret, for all is well. I have given you the power to move mountains. You will see them move. Trust Me, I do not lie. Lay all at My feet. My yoke is easy, My burden light. Cast all your cares upon Me. My love for you is deep. You are My delight! I love to hear your voice as you speak to Me. Open your heart, open your eyes, open your ears and Listen to what I am saying to you. Let My love flow to you and through you. Heed My voice, read My Word and come, follow Me.

11/07/2009
My child,
I have given you all I have. I have withheld nothing from you. What are you withholding from Me? I am here for you. Why do you not lay all at My feet? Trust Me, child, I am here. I do care about what is going on around you. I do care that you are hurting. Lay all at My feet and I shall lift you up. You are My beloved, child. Why would I not want to help you? My ways are not your ways but My way is best. Lean On Me, child. I shall carry you through all things. Come, sit with Me awhile. Allow Me to fill you. Allow Me to be your friend, your lover, your All in All. I love you, with a deep abiding love. Come to Me, all who are weak and heavy laden and I shall give thee rest.

11/20/2009
My child,
You have so much in store for you. Yes, life is an adventure. Yes, I have many surprises ahead. Remember to lean on Me. Remember to give all to Me and I will lighten the load. My ways are not your ways but you will understand, all will be revealed to you in time. I have laid the course before you. Do not hesitate to go ahead for all shall work to the good. Keep your eyes stayed on Me for I love you, child, with a deep abiding love and I will restore what the locusts have devoured. I shall raise up those from among you to do My will. Stand fast, stand firm in Me and you shall see many great and wondrous things come to pass. Trust Me, I do not lie. Rest in Me, allow Me to love you. Feel My peace wash over you as I cradle you in Mine arms.

12/06/2009
My child,
I am reaching out to you. Hold My hand for I shall take you places you have never gone. I will show you many great and wondrous things if you but trust Me. Look not to the right nor the left, follow Me and

Me alone, lean not to your own understanding. Those things that surround you are hindering your walk with Me but every obstacle shall be overcome. Lean on Me, child, I have you in the palm of My hand and nothing or no one can snatch you from Me. My ways are not easy but ALL will work to the good. I have chosen those who shall come forward. Know that I am with you. You are My beloved child in whom I am well pleased. Rest in Me child, rest in Me. Be still and know that I am God. The Alpha and Omega, the Beginning and the End.

12/23/2009

My child,

I am here for you. I have been waiting patiently for you to come to Me, I long to sup with you. You are My delight! All things will work together for good. Trust Me, leave all at My feet and all will go according to My plan. Many a heart shall feint with what is about to happen but I have called you. I shall raise you up in the last days. Be therefore assured, I have you in the palm of My hand. Do not worry nor fret for I am with you. My rod and My staff shall comfort you all the days of your life. Lean on Me, child, lean on Me for I am the King of Kings and Lord of Lords and I shall protect you. Go forth in boldness and tell them of Me and My love. The time grows short. Be still and know that I am God. I go before you to prepare the way.

01/05/2010

My child,

I love you. I am here for you. Seek Me always in all things for I have much to show you. All is not clear right now but soon you shall see that My hand is upon you and you shall bear much fruit. I am in no way displeased with you. Keep your eyes on Me and all will fall into place. I have chosen those who will stand by you because of Me and My love. They shall come forward to do My will in My timing. All will work together for good. Be not afraid to follow My lead. Do not worry about what man will say or do for I am in control. Stand fast, stand firm in Me for I am your All in All. Seek Me with your whole heart, mind and soul and ye shall find Me waiting with open arms, for you are My beloved child, in whom I am well pleased. Come, sit with Me awhile and let Me love you.

01/17/2010
My child,
I have much to say to you. You are Mine, bought with a price. I am your All in All. If you but look to Me, I will show you many great and wondrous things. I shall guide you in the way you should go. Lean on Me, I am your Stronghold. ALL, yes, ALL, will work to the good. Trust Me, child for I love thee with a deep abiding love. My heart cries with you when you are sad. My heart rejoices when you are glad. Keep your eyes on Me, child. Read My Word. Allow Me to speak to you. Allow Me to show you the answers to your questions. Be thou assured, I have you in the palm of My hand and I shall never leave you nor forsake you. Healing is yours, body, mind and spirit if you just look to Me. Forgive, for I have forgiven you. I will fill you to overflowing with My love, My peace and My joy unspeakable.

01/28/2010
My child,
I have given you many things to contemplate. I am revealing to you many truths. Open your eyes, open your ears, open your spirit to Me, for I wish to prepare you for what is to come. I will increase your wisdom and knowledge if you but look to Me. There is much going on you cannot see but I shall reveal to you what you need, when you need it. Trust Me, child, for I have a plan for you. Seek Me always, let Me show you the way you are to go. Be patient, child, for My timing is perfect. Allow My love to flow to you and through you. I shall reap the harvest in My time. Be steadfast in My Word. Your prayers waft up like a sweet smelling incense. Love Me, child, seek My face and Come, follow Me.

02/09/2010
My child,
I have not forgotten you, I hear your every prayer. Whenever you but say My Name, I am always there. Let me assure you, I will answer when

the time is right, just believe I hear. When the pattern is complete, the burden I will bear. My child, seek My face, put your hand in Mine. For, I shall sustain you, you and all mankind. Look to Me, My favored one, come boldly to My throne I have prepared a place for you, you and you alone. Your faith, has touched My heart, your faithfulness I see. Come, seek Me, child, spend some time with Me. My love for you is deep and rich, joy and peace are yours, eternally, Be still, My child, and seek My face, and come, now rest in Me.

02/25/2010

My child,

I have foreseen all that is happening around you. I am here for you. Lean on Me, child for I shall give you all the strength that you need. When you are weak, I am strong. Be still, child, turn to Me with all your heart, I will give you rest. My peace will go with you. My love will go with you. Your joy will be complete. You are My beloved, child. I have good things in store for you. All that I have is yours. I will show you the way if you just come to Me. My love for you is great, it is forever. Nothing or no one can snatch you from Me. My promises are True. Come to Me, child, talk to Me, I am listening. Then be still and let Me love you and whisper in your ear. Be not afraid, for I am the I AM. I am your Savior, Redeemer, Friend. You are Mine, bought with a price. Come, sit with Me awhile, allow Me to fill you to overflowing.

03/09/2010

My child,

You have seen many changes in this world. All seems to be out of control. No weapon formed against you shall prosper. Do not worry or be anxious, I am in control. All will work together for good for those who love Me and are called according to My purpose. I have called you, be not afraid. These things must happen. Keep your eyes on Me. Do not waiver. Do not turn to the right or to the left. Put yourself in My hands and I shall raise you up. My love for you is great. I would that none should perish but all have eternal life. Tell them of Me and My love. The time grows short. Let Me love you, child. Come sit with

Me. Allow Me to fill you to overflowing. Do not trust in the world or others. Trust in Me, for I am your All in All. Seek Me first in all things.

03/25/2010
My child,
I have delivered you from many things. My heart grows merry at the thought of you. You have given to Me, great joy! I see you struggle, but then you come to Me. You delight Me, child. You have been obedient to My Word. You have given all to Me and you hear My voice when I call. Be steadfast in your love for Me. Know that I love you with a deep abiding love. Know that you are the apple of My eye. Come to Me, when you are weak and heavy laden and I shall give you rest.

04/18/2010
My child,
I shall lift you up! Do not worry or fret, for I am with you. I go before you, child. Trust Me. All I have is yours. Be steadfast in your love for Me, for I have called you to a mighty work and I shall be with you and guide you. You do not have to have experience in what I am calling you to do, for I shall show you the way. You can do all things through Me. My rod and My staff shall comfort you all the days of your life. Keep your eyes on Me, child and I shall direct your path. I have heard your cry and the answer is on the way. Seek Me first in all things. I love you, child, with a deep abiding love. Lean not to your own understanding. Lean on me.

05/01/2010
My child,
Time is short. Look to Me in all things for I shall provide for you all that you need in the time ahead. I am preparing the way before you. Seek Me and My ways for I shall not fail you. All will work together for good. Trust Me, follow My lead. Look not to others, look to Me, for I am your All in All. I have a plan for you. Do not worry what people will think. My way is best. You will know that I have opened the door to a new beginning. Lean not to your own understanding. In all thy

ways acknowledge Me and I shall direct your path. Come to Me with all your burdens and lay them at My feet and I shall give you rest. I love you, child, with a deep abiding love. Come, sit with Me awhile.

05/13/2010
My child,
I have been beside you all the way. I will never leave you nor forsake you. Trust Me. I am preparing the way before you. Seek My face, always. Allow Me to be your All in All. All will work to the good. Meanwhile, lay all at My feet and rest in Me. My peace, I give you. I will take you through this desert. Hold onto that which is good. Let go of the things of this world for I shall supply all your needs. My love for you is deep. Allow Me to love you. I have anointed you from on High to do My bidding. I am well pleased. Rest awhile and listen to My voice and Come, follow Me.

05/23/2010
My child,
I love you. I have called you by name to do My bidding. You have surrendered all to Me. All I have is yours. You have but to ask, believing and you shall receive. The time grows short. There is much for you to do. In all your ways acknowledge Me and I shall direct your path. I know you do not understand why those things are going on around you. There is a purpose for all things. All will work together for good. Trust Me, child, for I shall give you the victory. Lean not to your own understanding, lean on Me. My heart cries for those who will not listen. Tell them, tell them of Me and My love. Let not your heart be troubled for you are the apple of My eye. You are My beloved child. Come, sit with Me awhile and let Me love you.

06/03/2010
My child,
I await our time together. You are such a joy to Me. Open your heart, open your mind to what I would say to you. You are My beloved child. You are the apple of My eye. You have been chosen, child. Go forth with

boldness and tell those who will listen of Me and My love. Show them, by example, the way. Allow Me to love through you. Allow all the fruit to come forth in your life. It warms My heart to see how faithful you have been even in times of trouble. You have perservered and trusted Me. I shall not fail you, child, for I am with you always. I shall be your Shield and Buckler. Know My love for you is deep and I shall supply all your needs. Trust Me, child, I know what you are going through and I am with you. Breathe deep and let My peace wash over you.

06/15/2010
My child,
I am always here for you. Bring all to Me for I have the answers. I am preparing the way before you. Seek Me first in all things. Yes, I have heard your prayers and petitions. Yes, I shall answer. Leave all at My feet and I shall supply all that you need. My timing is perfect. Wait on Me for I am preparing the way. Hearts are changing, you will see the fruit of your prayers soon. Keep your eyes on Me and Trust Me and many miracles will come to pass. My yoke is easy, My burden light. Bask in My peace as you allow Me to work in your life. You are My beloved child and all things will work together for good. Feel My love as I wrap you in Mine arms. Let My joy well up within you for My joy is your strength. Lean on Me, child, lean on Me. I am your All in All.

06/26/2010
My child,
I shall lift you up! Do not worry or fret for I am with you. I go before you, child, trust Me. All I have is yours. Be steadfast in your love for Me, for I have called you to a mighty work, and I shall be with you and guide you. You do not have to have experience in what I am calling you to do for I shall show you the way. You can do all things through Me. My rod and My staff shall comfort you all the days of your life. Keep your eyes on Me, child, and I shall direct your path. I have heard your cry and the answer is on the way. Seek Me first in all things. I love you, child with a deep abiding love. Lean not to your own understanding, lean on Me.

07/07/2010

My child,

You have given to Me great joy! I love the sweet smelling incense of your prayers and praises. My heart grows heavy with those who will not listen. I call to them and they do not hear Me for they are consumed by this world. They are fearful. If only they would come to Me and lay their burdens at My feet I would set them free. Tell them, child, of Me and My love. Show them the way. Stand fast, stand firm in Me, child, for there will be a shaking as the wheat is separated from the chaff. Be not afraid for I love you with a deep abiding love and nothing or no one can snatch you from Me. I am with you always, even unto the end of the age. Keep your eyes on Me, child, for I shall supply all your needs. Do not worry about what you should eat or drink or what you shall wear, I am your Provider. Rest in Me, child rest in Me.

07/16/2010

My child,

I have given you a great gift. Use it for My glory. Be not afraid to go forth in My Name and do My bidding. I have prepared the way before you. I have given you the ability, now, walk in My way. I shall reveal to you all you need to know for this new endeavor. I have prepared you for this task. You are ready, if you completely trust in Me. I have imparted My wisdom and you have been anointed from on High. I will work through you. Seek Me first in all things and all will work to the good. Trust Me, child, for I love you with a deep abiding love. The love, peace and joy I give to you, freely give to others as you minister in My Name. Lean on Me, child, you can do all things through Me. I am opening a new realm, walk in it!

07/27/2010

My child,

Why do you doubt Me, child? I have you in the palm of My hand. I will never leave you nor forsake you. Trust Me, My Word is True. I give but good gifts to My children. I did not say the way would be easy but I will be with you all the way. I shall supply all your needs.

There are those things which you think you need, but you do not. Ask, believing and you shall receive. My Word is True. Seek and you shall find, knock and the door shall be opened unto you. My Word is True, I do not lie. Do not doubt, child. Trust Me with all your heart and lean not to your own understanding. In all your ways acknowledge Me and I shall direct your path. My yoke is easy, My burden light. Know that you are the apple of My eye. You are My delight!

The following are the latest Words I have received. If you are interested in receiving a copy of the Words I receive from time to time please send me an e mail with WORD in the subject line and I will add you to my list. smjpray@aol.com

Thank you,
Serena

10/4/2022
My child,
I have given you all that you need to go forth in My name and be a witness. You have come before Me with praise and thanksgiving. You have given all to Me, therefore I will give all to you. Ask, believing and you shall receive, knock and the door shall be opened unto you. I shall supply all your needs. My ways are not your ways, acknowledge Me, and I shall direct your path. You are Mine, My beloved, and I am yours. Be steadfast in your love for Me. Rejoice!, for I have healed you and set you free. Healing is not only physical, I see all your needs. Let My love permeate your entire being and bring you peace. I must come first, but you must choose that path.

smj

10/14/2022
My child,
My love for you is never ending. I long to speak to you day and night. I have gone ahead and opened some doors. Be not afraid to walk through

them. You will know I have ordained what is happening. You shall see My power manifest. It will bring you great joy! My heart is with you. Hold Me tight. Come to Me all ye who are weary and heavy laden and I will give you rest. My yoke is easy, My burden light.. Seek Me first in all things. I covet the time we spend together. Your praise and prayers are sweet smelling incense.

Let not your heart be troubled for I am with you. Allow Me full reign, I shall remove all the hindrances that try to deter you from doing what I have called you to. Be still and know that I am God.

smj

10/28/2022
My child,
I have given you all that you need to go forth in My Name and do My bidding. I have called you to this time. I will show you what I have in store for you. Look to Me in all things. Mine eyes go to and fro from all the earth. I see all that is happening. There are so many who will not listen. But you, child, listen to My voice and follow Me. I am your Redeemer, Savior, Deliverer. I am your All in All. Let Me love you. Let Me lead you by My Spirit. Receive all that I have for you, for you are Mine, bought with a price. My love for you is eternal.

smj

I AM WITH THEE

You will know that I am with thee
You will see Me in the clouds
I shall be your Consolation
Every minute, every hour.

Keep your eyes upon Me, Jesus And
I will show you how
To practice what I'm preaching So
that I can use you now.

Every knee shall bow every tongue
confess that I am Lord
I am with you even though there will be discord
Follow Me, As I will lead you
Thus saith the Lord

I am with thee, I am with thee
Many gifts and promises don't deny
On My Word, you can rely

I am with thee, I am with thee
All the sins of My people
Only make Me cry.

As My tears do turn to gladness
. . . . This can be
For if you tell them of salvation I
will draw them unto Me.

ACKNOWLEDGMENTS INDEX

Page 1141: From the book WITH MY WHOLE HEART by Karen Burton Mains. Copyright © 1987 by Multnomah Press. Published by Multnomah Press, Portland, Oregon 97266. Used by permission.

Page 1143: Taken from A WOMAN'S CHOICE by Eugenia Price. Copyright © 1962 by Eugenia Price. Published by Zondervan Bible Publishers. Used by permission.

Page 1148: By Rosemary Jensen. Copyright © 1990 by The Zondervan Corporation.

Page 1151: Taken from MEMORIES by Kathryn Hillen. Copyright © 1987 by Kathryn Hillen. Used by permission of Zondervan Publishing House.

Page 1153: By Jill Briscoe. Copyright © 1990 by The Zondervan Corporation.

Page 1155: Taken from Luke 1:46-50.

Page 1156: Taken from BE STILL AND KNOW by Millie Stamm. Copyright © 1978 by Millie Stamm. Used by permission of Zondervan Publishing House.

Page 1159: By Rosalind Rinker. Copyright © 1990 by The Zondervan Corporation.

Page 1169: By Gloria Gaither. Copyright © 1990 by Gloria Gaither.